T0198814

THE DR. WILLIAMS' CHORD CHEMISTRY

THE MASTER'S GUITAR BOOK

VOLUME II

William   Mohele

Order this book online at www.trafford.com
or email orders@trafford.com

Most Trafford titles are also available at major online book retailers.

Printed in the United States of America.

ISBN: 978-1-4669-5091-7 (sc)
ISBN: 978-1-4669-5090-0 (e)

Trafford rev. 08/20/2012

 www.trafford.com

North America & international
toll-free: 1 888 232 4444 (USA & Canada)
phone: 250 383 6864 ♦ fax: 812 355 4082

INTRODUCTION

We have tried in the first volume of this work to lay the foundation of this new guitar method by introducing the guitarist to new words, new ways of conceiving, understanding and memorizing chords.

In this second volume, the guitarist will use all those previous knowledge to comprehend the new chapters in order to master his instrument and try to be as good as the best rhythm guitarists in the world.

Examples have therefore been taken from some of the best guitarists in the world to illustrate most of the concepts described here.

Some pretty interesting topics and chapters that are not found in most guitar books are described here for the first time, in a simple and comprehensible way, as: THE MODULATION and EXTERNAL CHORDS.

Enjoy the addictive book.

The author.

FOREWORD

We wish to warn the reader on the fact that this book is very different from the other books published on the topic.

Many "traditional concepts" on chords have been completely changed (example: open chords).

The new and unusual way many "technical" words are used in this work is only binding on the author and done with the sole intention of making the book as didactic as possible.

Unlike most chord dictionaries:

1. The majority of chords are described in C.

2. The other chords that are not in C are mentioned to show some particular (unusual) fingerings among chords of the same group.

3. Most chords are described in a regrouped way and displayed together on a single fingerboard hence making easier a global understanding and memorization of chords.

This concept of chord regrouping into two different main groups, of similar construction and sound, each made up of three sub-groups, allows a better , faster and more practical understanding of chords after working out similarities in their construction, fingering and sonority.

4. The chord diagrams (on the fingerboards) often appear in double , and roman numerals are used as explained in pages18 and 19 of the volume 1.

TABLE OF CONTENTS

CHAP.I CHORDS OF THE ALTERED MODES

I.ALTERED 7TH CHORDS

These are **7th chords** whose fifth note (**5**) and/or ninth note (**9**) has been « **altered** » meaning, **"sharpened"** or **"flattened"**.

This définition also includes **extensions of the 7th chord** namely **the 9th and 13th chords** (the11th chord being excluded for obvious reasons).

These altered **7th chords** are in most cases **"resolved" 7th chords**.

A 7th chord is called "resolved" when it is followed by another chord (major or minor) built a fourth higher meaning, whose root note is located at 2 tones and a half higher.

Therefore, it will be possible to alter any **7th** or **9th** or **13th** chord, if the chord played afterwards has its root note located at 2,5 tones higher.

Examples:

- For **B7** followed by **Em**, it will be possible to play: **B7$^{\#}$9** followed by **Em**
- For **G7** followed by **CM7**, it will be possible to play: **G13$^{\flat}$9** followed by **CM7**
- For **A7** followed by **D7**, it will be possible to play: **A7$^{\#}$5** followed by **D7**

It is a technique widely used in jazz, funk and modern blues.

The guitarist will therefore have to identify these resolved 7th chords in a given chord progression and then, alter them according to the desired sound effect.

It has to be said here that the lead guitarist will be able to take widely advantage of this concept and its applications, to « improvise » with « altered modes » (altered mode , diminished mode,whole tone scale,etc…) on these altered chords.

C7^b5 (1, 3, ^b5, 7) or C7⁻⁵

The basic chord is the dominant **7th** whose fifth (**5**) will be « flattened ».

A. HARMONICS : The strummed chords are inversions.
Possibility of playing a Root position form by using the flowing arpeggio technique.

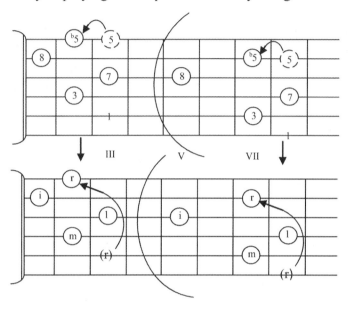

Notice the use, in « two steps », of the ring finger with the flowing arpeggio technique.

* At the end of the neck :

Harmonic = **B7^b5**

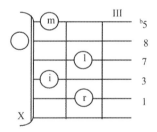

Grand harmonic = **G7^b5**

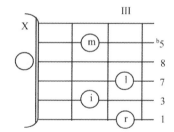

George Benson performing live at the National Indoor Arena,
Birmingham, UK on June 28 2008

* INVERSIONS :

Harm.: Top note= **7**

Harm.: Top note =ᵇ**5**

Gᵈ harm.: Top note= **3**
(possible flowing arp. to play in root pos.)

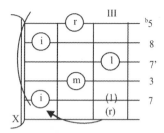
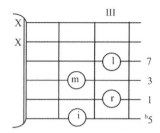
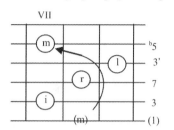

* Possibility of flowing arp. to play
  in root position

B. BARRES : Most used shapes, played strummed, with a very «jazzy» sound.

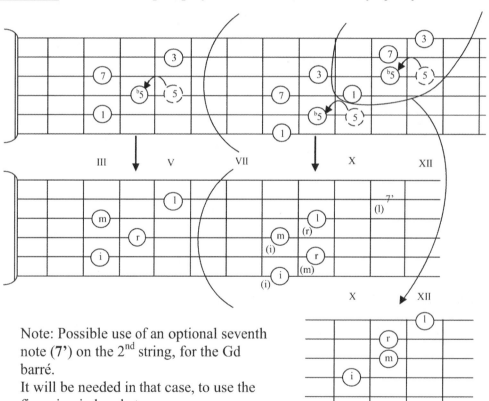

Note: Possible use of an optional seventh
note (**7'**) on the 2ⁿᵈ string, for the Gd
barré.
It will be needed in that case, to use the
fingering in brackets.

* At the end of the neck:

Barré = **A7^{b}5**

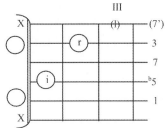

Gd Barré = **E7^{b}5**

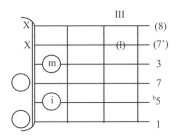

Sm Barré = **D7^{b}5**

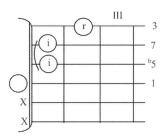

Possibility of playing
another 7th note (**7'**) on
the first string (l)

Possibility of doubling the
7th note(7),with the finger
1,and the note 1(8) on the
1st string.

* Opened chord:

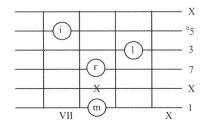

or

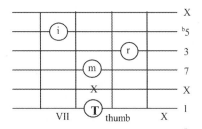

* Inversions : top note = flat fifth (^{b}5)

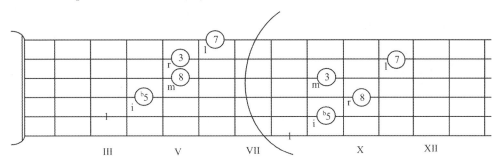

* Other Grand barré inversion

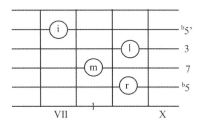

6

C9^{b}5 (1, 3, ^{b}5, 7, 9)

The basic chord is naturally the **9th** chord.

A. HARMONICS :

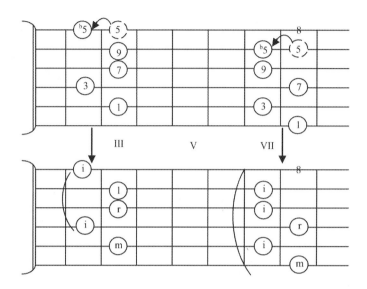

* At the end of the neck :

Grand harmonic : **F9^{b}5**

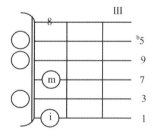

B. BARRES

These are Grand barré opened chord shapes

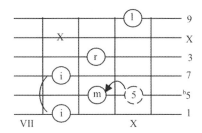

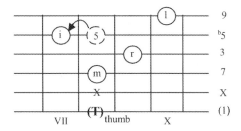

Possible use of the thumb (T) to finger the root note (1).

* INVERSIONS :

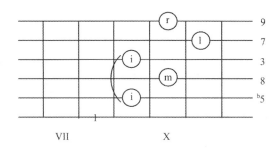

Derived from the Grand Barré

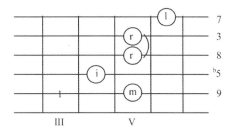

Derived from the Barré

C 13^b5 (1, 3, ^b5, 7, 9, 13)

These are **13th** barré chords with « flat » fifth.

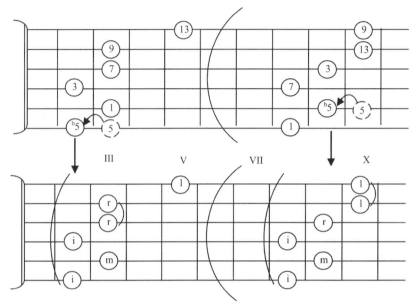

Note:
The flat fifth (^b5) is the top note for the barré.

These chords are rather difficult to finger.

Small barré

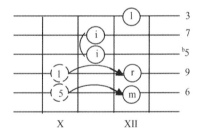

Chord without root note.

* At the end of the neck : Grand barré = **E 13^b5**

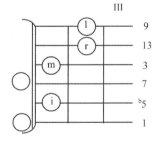

Inversion without root note(harmonic)

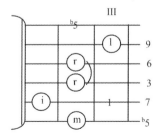

C 7^{b}5^{b}9 (1, 3, ^{b}5, 7, ^{b}9)

Derived from the chord C 9^{b}5

A. HARMONICS :

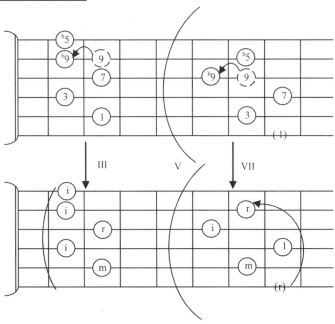

III   V   VII

Remark:
The Grand Harmonic chord is
played in Root position only with
the help of the flowing arpeggio.

B. BARRES :

No Root Position chord.

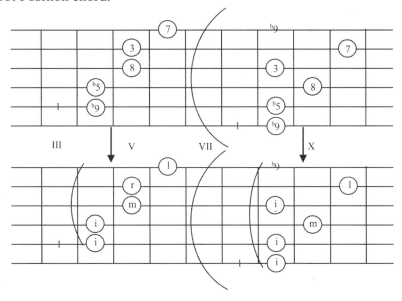

Top note = ^{b}9

* Grand barré with ^b**5** as top note :

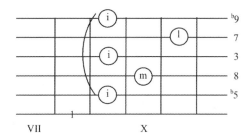

* Grand barré with **7** as top note :

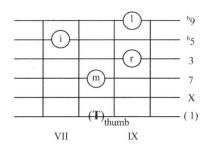

Inversion with possible use of the thumb
to finger the root note(1) = opened chord.

Do 13^{b}5^{b}9   (1, 3, ^{b}5, 7, ^{b}9, 13)

No Root position chord.

A. HARMONICS :

Harmonic and Small harmonic

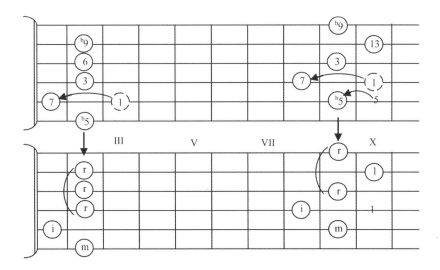

B. Barrés :

Barré and Grand Barré

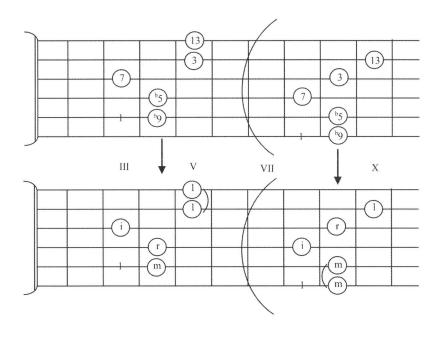

C7^b5[#]9 (1, 3, ^b5, 7, [#]9)

Basic chord = **C9^b5** whose ninth note (**9**) has been "sharpened".
These chords are constructed, here, with the harmonic shapes only.

HARMONIC AND GRAND HARMONIC :

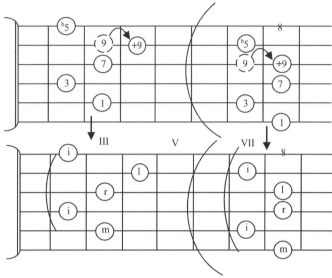

* INVERSIONS : Top note = ^b5

Harmonic and Small Harmonic

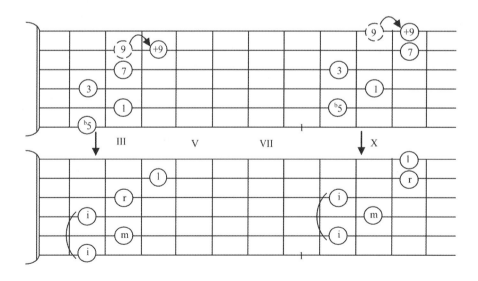

C 7^{b}5^{b}9$^\#$9(1, 3, ^{b}5, 7, ^{b}9, $^\#$9)

No Root position chord.
The basic chord is the previous **C 7^{b}5$^\#$9** to which has been added a ^{b}**9** note.

A. HARMONICS

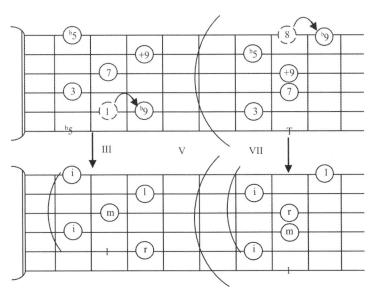

* At the end of the neck :

Grand harmonic : **F 7^{b}5^{b}9$^+$9**

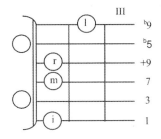

B. BARRES :

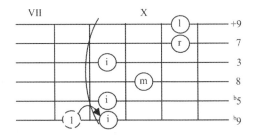

C7#5 (1, 3, #5, 7)

Basic chord = **dominant seventh** of which all the fifth notes have been « sharpened ».

A. HARMONICS: The Root position form is only played with the help of the flowing arpeggio.

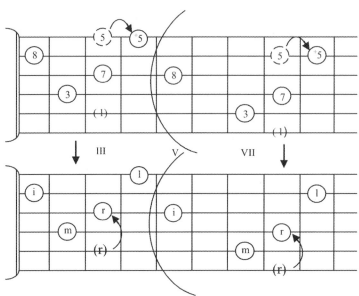

* At the end of the neck:

Harmonic =**B7#5**

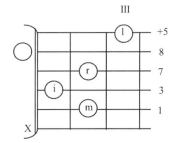

Grand harmonic = **G7#5**

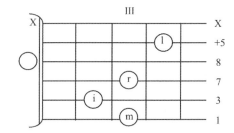

* INVERSIONS : Top note = Seventh (**7**)

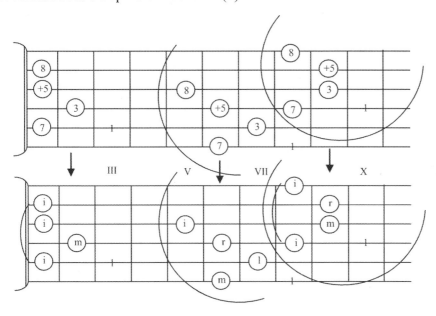

B. BARRES :

We are going to have double augmented fifth notes (**+5**) for the Barré and Grand barré.

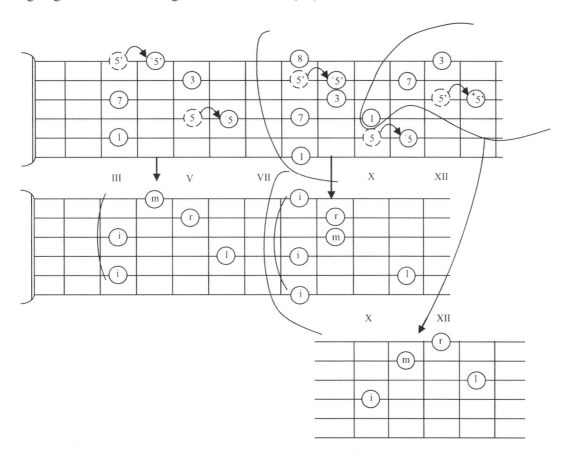

* At the end of the neck

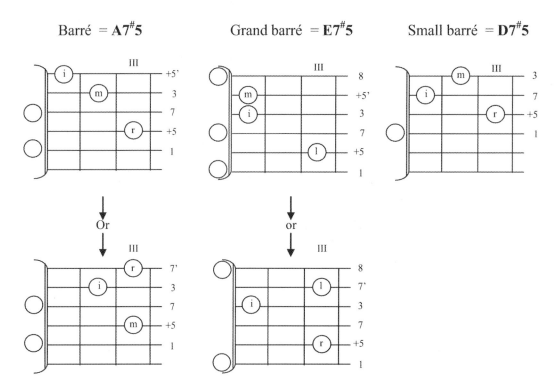

Barré = **A7#5**   Grand barré = **E7#5**   Small barré = **D7#5**

Or   or

* Opened chord : of very "Jazzy" sound, especially for the Grand Barré .

Barré   Grand barré

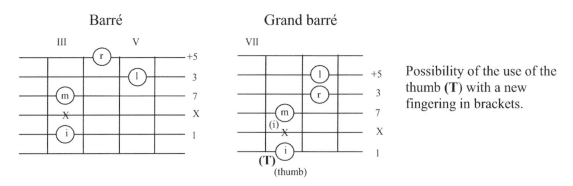

Possibility of the use of the thumb **(T)** with a new fingering in brackets.

* INVERSIONS :

Top note = augmented fifth (**+5**)
Bottom note = seventh (**7**)

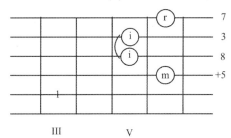
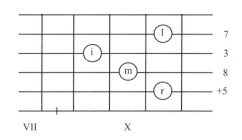

C 9#5 (1, 3, #5, 7, 9)

Ninth chord whose fifth has been augmented (#5).

A. HARMONICS :

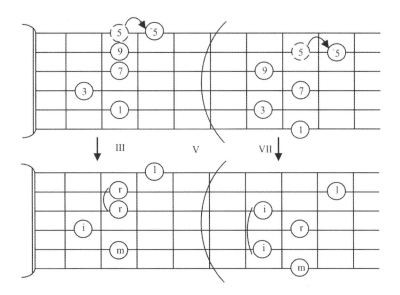

* At the end of the neck:

Grand Harmonic = **F9#5**

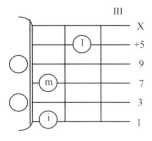

B. BARRES : Only the opened Grand barré is a " Root position " chord.

* Grand barré :

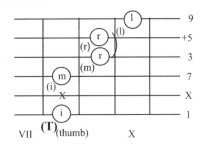

Possibility of involving the thumb **(T)** which will give the fingering in brackets. Obvious « Jazzy » sonority.

* Barré : Top note = **+5**

At the end of the neck, in **A**, it becomes a root position chord

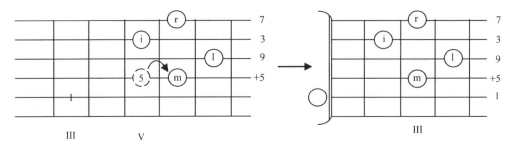

* Small Barré

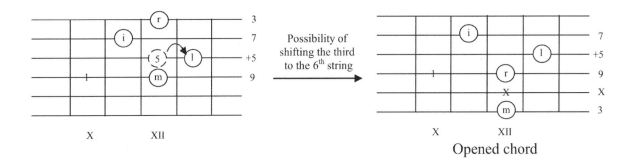

Possibility of shifting the third to the 6th string

Opened chord

C 7$^{\#}$5^{b}9 (1, 3, $^{\#}$5, 7, ^{b}9)

The basic chord will be the previous one (**C 9$^{\#}$5**) with the **ninth** note « **flattened** » (^{b}9).

A. HARMONICS :

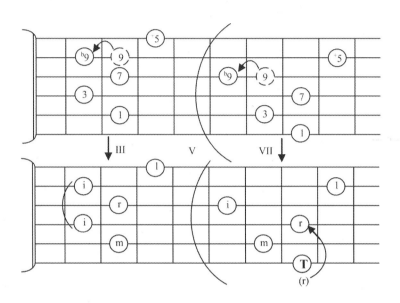

Note the use of the thumb(**T**) to finger the root note, and the possible use of the flowing arpeggio instead of involving the thumb, for the Gd harmonic(r).

B. BARRE : Only the Grand Barré has an interesting sound.
Its « opened » form is of a rather «jazzy» sound.

C 7[#]5[#]9 (1, 3, [#]5, 7, [#]9)

The basic chord is still the **C 9[#]5** chord but this time the **ninth** note is "sharpened"
([#]9 = ^b3).

A. HARMONICS

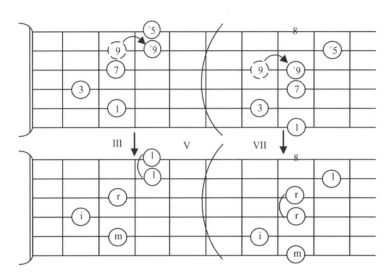

* At the end of the neck :

Grand harmonic = **F 7[#]5[#]9**

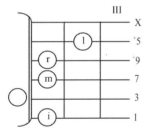

* INVERSION : in D7[#]5[#]9

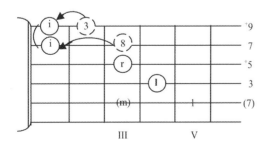

The third has been "flattened" to get the note
⁺9 (or ^b3), while the seventh note (7) is got by
lowering the root note in octave (8) by a tone.
Note the possibility of doubling the note 7 with
the finger **m.**

B. BARRES : only the Grand barré chord is in "Root position".

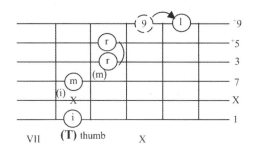

In brackets, other possible fingering.

* **INVERSION : Barré**

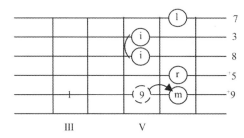

C 7#5b9#9 (1, 3, #5, 7, b9, #9)

We can consider it to be a **7#5** chord, to which the notes **b9** and **#9** have been added.

A. HARMONICS:

The only interesting chord is the Grand Harmonic in root position.

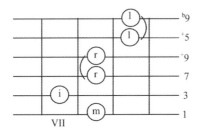

Chord difficult to play because of the required inflexion of the small finger (l).

B. BARRES : Barré and Grand barré without root notes.

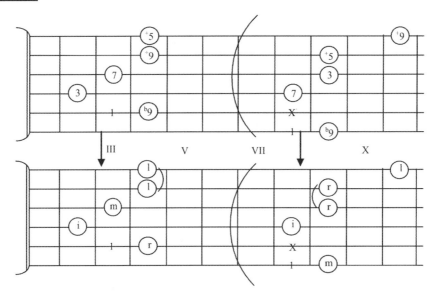

C 7^{b}9 (1, 3, 5, 7, ^{b}9)

We will consider it to be a **ninth chord** whose ninth note (9) has been "flattened" into a ^{b}9.
Important remark: Any **7^{b}9** chord without root note is equal to the diminished chord built a semi tone lower (here **C$^#$dim**.)

A. HARMONICS :

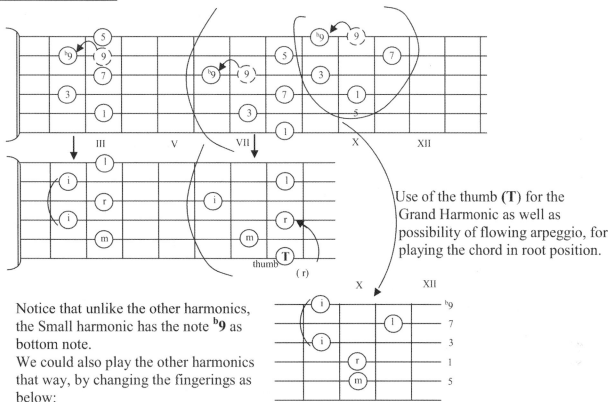

Use of the thumb **(T)** for the Grand Harmonic as well as possibility of flowing arpeggio, for playing the chord in root position.

Notice that unlike the other harmonics, the Small harmonic has the note ^{b}9 as bottom note.
We could also play the other harmonics that way, by changing the fingerings as below:

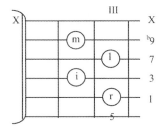

Harmonic

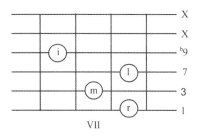

Grand Harmonic

* INVERSIONS :

Harmonic

Grand harmonic

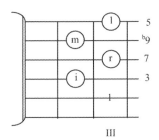

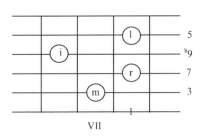

B. BARRES :

No Root position chord apart from the Grand Barré.
The chord requires a strong muscular tension of the small finger.

Grand Barré :

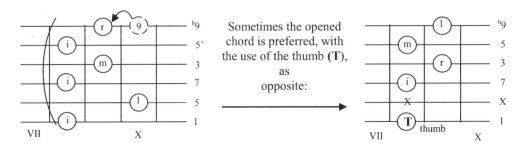

Sometimes the opened chord is preferred, with the use of the thumb (**T**), as opposite:

Practical and movable fingerings for all the Barré shapes will be those with the root note replaced by the note **♭9** (= Top note) as below:

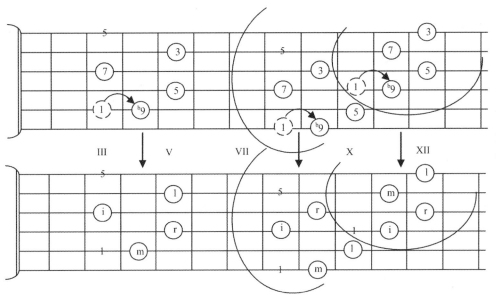

Note the shape resemblance to the diminished 7th chord (see page 35).

* Each of these Barré inversions could give an opened chord of identical "morphology", but with different (specific) note distributions, as regards the top and bottom notes, as below:

Barré :

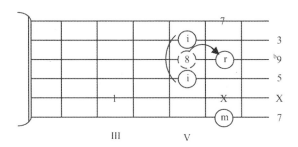

This chord is derived from the "panoramic" inversion as one can notice, with as top note, the seventh (**7**).

Grand barré	**Small Barré**
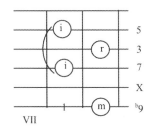	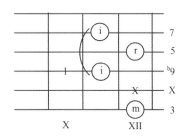
Top note = **♭9**	Top note = **3**

* Other inversions

Barré	**Grand barré**	**Small barré**
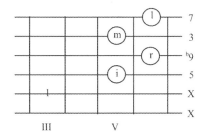	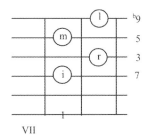	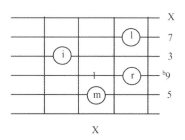

C 13^{b}9 (1, 3, 5, 7, ^{b}9, 13)

13th chord whose ninth note has been " flattened'(^{b}9)

A. HARMONICS

Harmonic

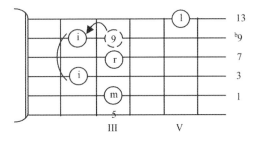

Grand harmonic

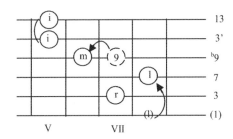

The strummed chord is an inversion, with the third **(3)** as top note while the flowing arpeggio technique allows to play the chord in Root position.

✱ **At the end of the neck**

Grand harmonic = **G 13^{b}9**

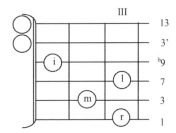

* Opened chord : Grand Harmonic

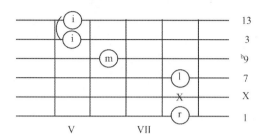

Chord difficult to strum, reserved
for guitarists with long fingers.

* INVERSIONS : Top note = 7

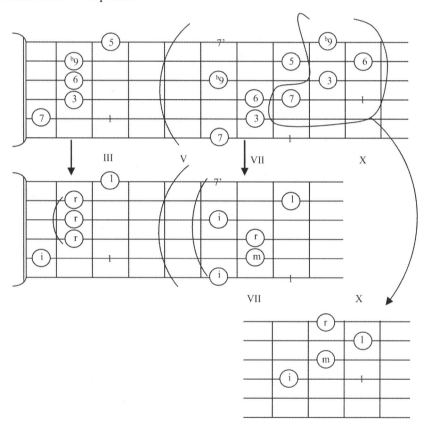

B. BARRES : The only Root position chord is the Grand Barré, played with the thumb (**T**).
The others are « opened » inversions.

Grand barré

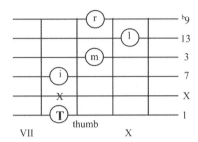

* INVERSIONS : The root note is raised by a semi tone.

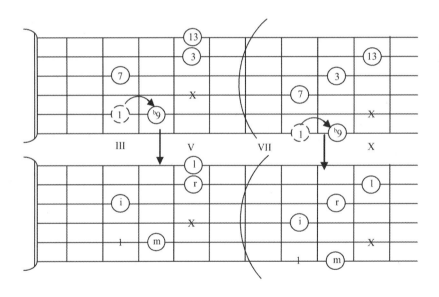

The sound obtained is very "Jazzy".

* Other opened inversion

Barré :

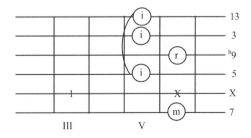

This chord derives, of course, from the "panoramic" inversion.

C7#9 (1, 3, 5, 7, #9)

The **9th chord** could be taken as basic chord .It will then be enough to just « sharpen » its ninth note to get the new **7#9** chord.

A. HARMONICS :

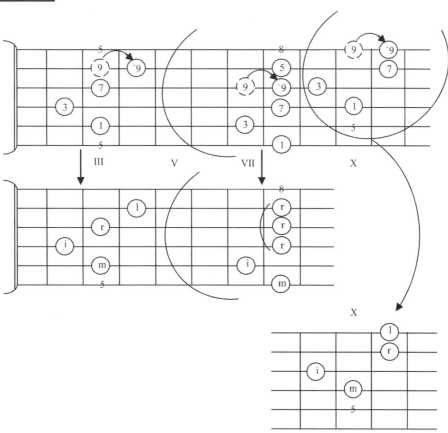

* Opened chords :

The optional fifth above (on the 6th string for the Harmonic and the 5th string for the Small Harmonique) is used in their construction.

Harmonic

Small Harmonic

B. BARRES : We will only mention the Grand barré chord and its inversion.

.

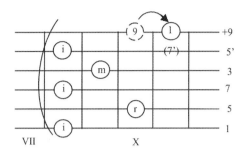

Note the possibility of adding a second seventh note (**7'**) on the second string, fretted with the little finger (l),for the guitarist with long fingers.

* At the end of the neck : **E 7#9**

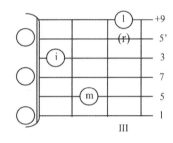

The additional seventh note (**7'**) can, here, be added with the aid of the annular (r).

* **INVERSION :**

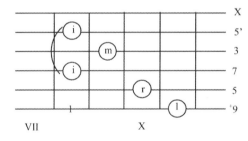

C 7^{b}9$^#$9 (1, 3, 5, 7, ^{b}9, $^#$9)

This chord can be considered as a **7$^#$9** chord to which a **^{b}9** note has been added .
Only the Grand Harmonic will be a " Root position " chord.

A. HARMONICS :

Grand harmonic

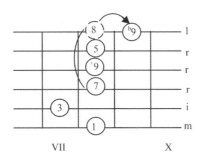

The root note in octave (**8**) is "sharpened" =
^{b}9.
Chord with indisputable "Jazzy" sound,
involving all the 6 strings.
Note: The position of fingers(fingering) is
indicated, here, next to the chord diagram.

Harmonic

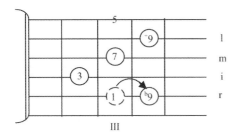

The root note is "sharpened" to get the
note **^{b}9**.

Other harmonic

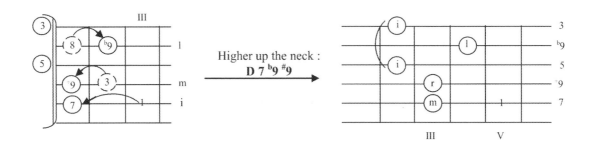

Higher up the neck :
D 7 ^{b}9 $^#$9

B. BARRES

Barré and Grand barré

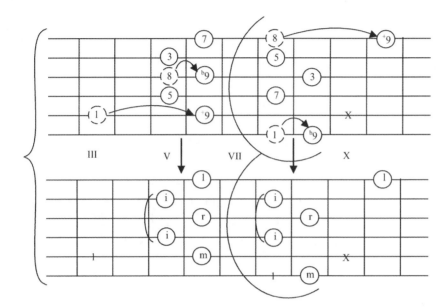

Comments:

1. The Barré chord is derived from the «panoramic inversion». Its $^+9$ note comes from the raise of the root note (**1**) by one and a half tone, while the $^b9$ comes from the raise of the root in octave (**8**) by a semi tone.

2. With the Grand barré chord, alterations also of the root note (**1**) and of the root-octave (**8**) but in a reversed way.
The Grand barré is here, an « opened » chord.

Small barré

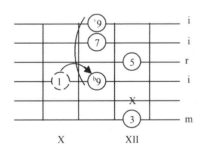

Brian May of Queen performs with the top 6 contestants onstage at
FOX's 'American Idol' Season 11 Top 6 Live Performance
Show on April 25, 2012 in Hollywood, California

Diminished C (1, ^b3, ^b5, 6)

Chord of minor composition by definition, however considered, depending on the authors, either as a **7th** chord whose notes, apart from the root note, have been "flattened" or as a **7th** chord whose root note has been "sharpened".
It is so used as a substitution chord of some major or altered chords.

It will be widely used by the jazz guitarist either as a passing chord (between two chords) or as a substitute chord for a simple **7th** chord or a **7^b9** chord (see chapter on chord substitution).

This chord has a particular structure: there is an interval of a minor third (meaning one and a half tone) between all the four notes which compose it.

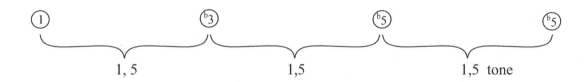

This special structure is going to give to the chord two particular characteristics:

1. The chord <u>repeats itself at **every 4 frets**</u> on the guitar keyboard (up or downwards the keyboard).

2. Every note composing the chord gives its name to the chord, what amounts to saying that every note in the chord can be considered as the chord's root note.

All the chords described below derive from the "Barré" shapes.
We chose, arbitrarily, to construct them by considering them to be **7th** chords whose notes, except the root note, were flattened.

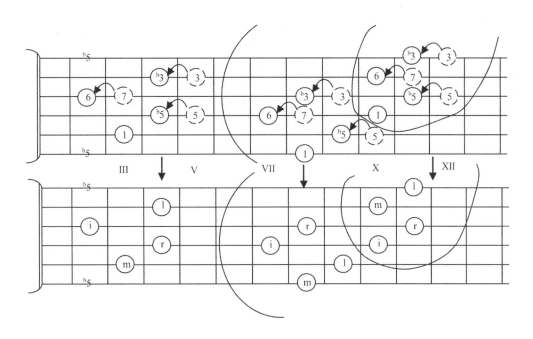

* Other Grand Barré chord :

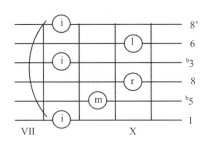

Chord with a very interesting sound, involving all the **6** strings on the fingerboard.

* Chords of the end of the neck:

Gd barré N^O1 = **E dim.**   Gd barré N^O2 = **F dim.**   Sm barré = **D dim.**

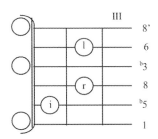 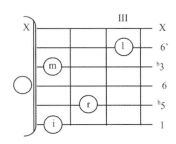 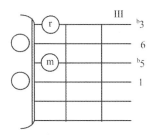

* Opened Chords :

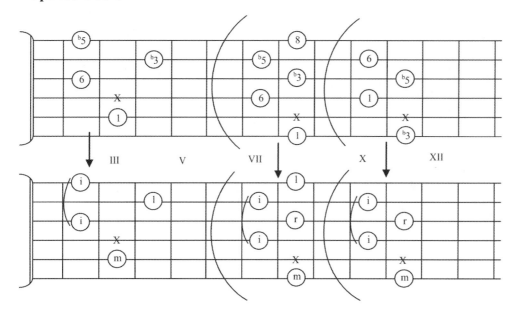

II.ALTERED M7 CHORDS

CM7 [#]5 (1, 3, [#]5, M7)

This chord is used by some modern jazz guitarists, in **harmonic position I**, when the lead guitarist is improvising with the **harmonic minor mode** or the **Ionian#5 mode** (see books on modes).

A. HARMONICS :

The basic chord will be the **M7,** whose fifth will be augmented **(+5)**

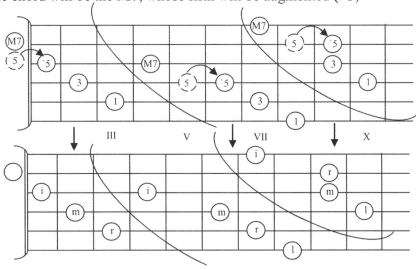

* **Other fingerings :**

Harmonic : up the
neck = **D M7#5**

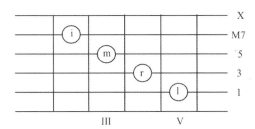

Small harmonic
(end of the neck): **F M7#5**

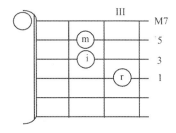

B. BARRES :

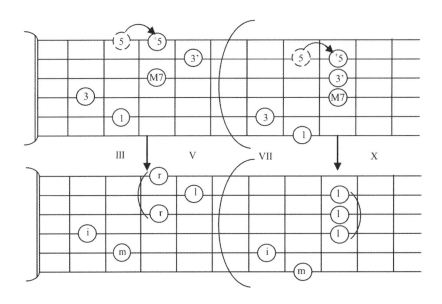

III   V   VII   X

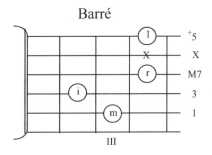
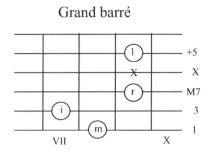

* Opened chords :

Barré

Grand barré

III

VII   X

III. MINOR CHORDS

CmM7 (1, ^b3, 5, M7)

Chord of harmonic position I for pieces played in a minor key (scale), peculiar to some music styles (extremely rare in the jazz, blues and stemming styles, which are played in the major key).

We will consider it, in the Jazz, as a **M7** chord whose third has been "flattened" into a ^b**3.**

A. HARMONICS :

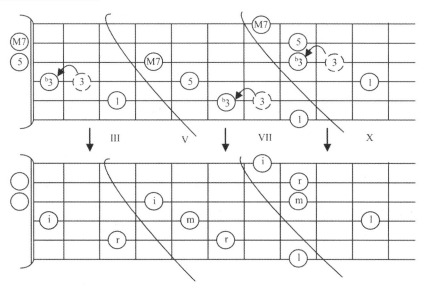

These harmonic shapes are difficult to play because requiring a strong stretching of the fingers.

To be tried by guitarists with long fingers.

* Other fingerings :

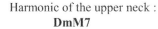

Harmonic of the upper neck :
DmM7

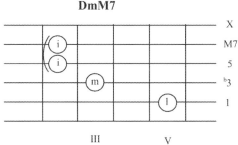

Sm harm.(end of the neck)=
FmM7

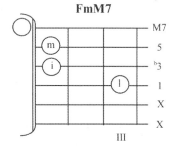

B. BARRES

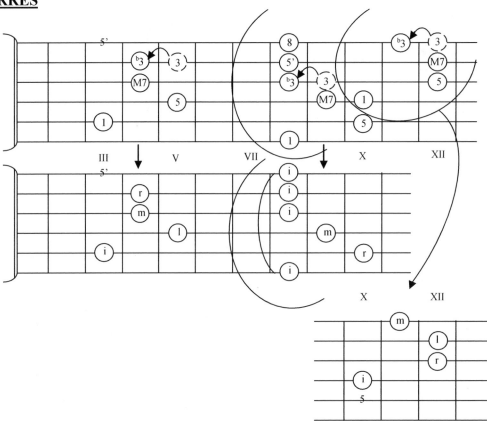

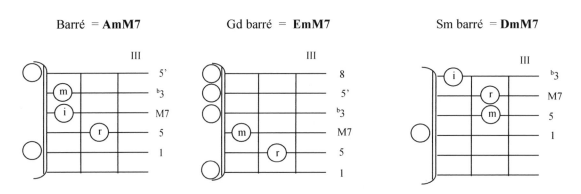

* At the end of the neck :

Barré = **AmM7**   Gd barré = **EmM7**   Sm barré = **DmM7**

Remark: These chords can be used in a major key as passing chords,
during the transition from **IV** to **I** or from **IIm** towards **IV**,
like this: - **IVM7** → **IVmM7** → **I**
              - **II m** → **IImM7** → **IV**

Cm9^b5 (1, ^b3, ^b5, 7, 9)

Chord played in harmonic position **VII** on a **locrian⌐2 mode** (played by the lead guitarist).
The basic chord will be the **m9** chord whose fifth has been "flattened".
The only chord "strummed" in Root position will be the Grand barré one.

A. HARMONICS :

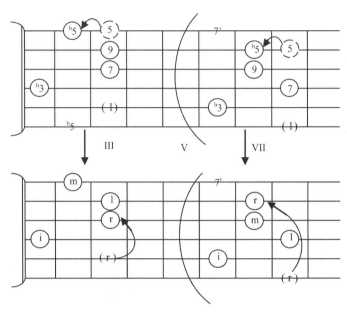

Strummed chords are inversions. However, the flowing arpeggio technique could allow to play them in arpeggio by beginning with their root note (Root position).

* The Small harmonic

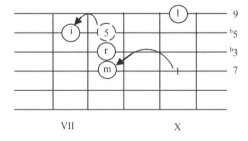

* At the end of the neck :

Harmonic = **Bm9ᵇ5**

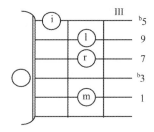

Small harmonic = **Fm9ᵇ5**

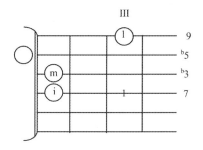

* Opened chord : Harmonic

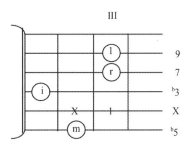

B. BARRES :

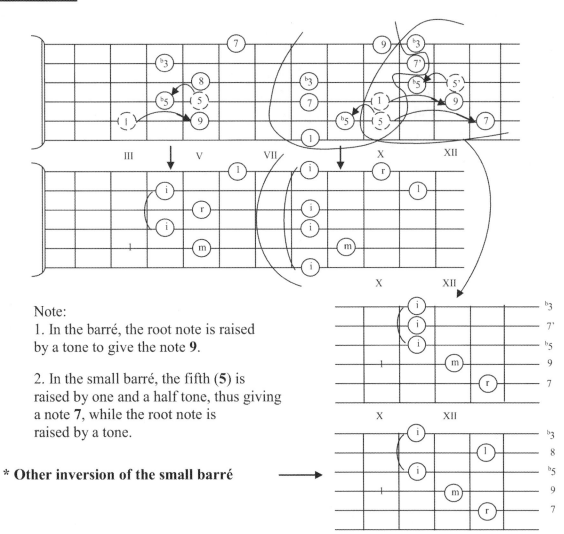

Note:

1. In the barré, the root note is raised by a tone to give the note **9**.

2. In the small barré, the fifth (**5**) is raised by one and a half tone, thus giving a note **7**, while the root note is raised by a tone.

* **Other inversion of the small barré** ⟶

* **At the end of the neck :**

Grand barré = **Em9^b5**

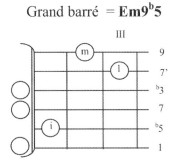

* Opened chord :

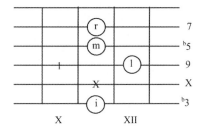

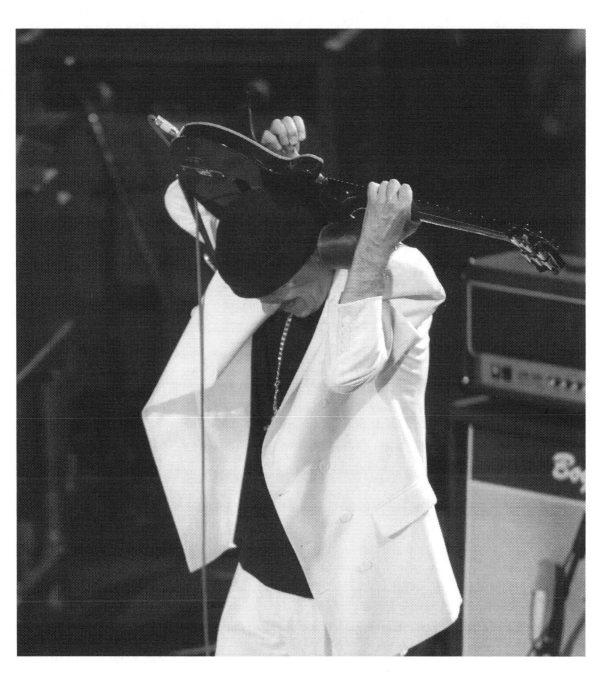

Carlos Santana plays the guitar behind his head during his
performance at the 5th annual Latin Grammy Awards
at the Shrine Auditorium in Los Angeles, 01

CHAP . II <u>THE MODULATION</u>

A modulation can simply be defined as the transition from one key to another during the execution (or sometimes at the end) of a music piece.
The jazz guitarist can even modulate more than once in the same piece.

<u>Example</u>: Modulation from the key of C to F and from the key of F, return towards that of C.

|| C (M7) | Am (7) | Dm (7) | Gm (7) - C7 | F (M7) | Dm (7) - G7 | C (M7).....
  I (C)   VIm (C)   IIm (C)   IIm (F) V7(F) I(F)   IIm (C) V7(C) I (C)

We have said, while speaking about the harmonic function of chords (page 88-89, volume I), that the major chords of a key (I, IV, and V), constituted the <<pillars.>> of the said key.
This truth is going to find all its importance in the modulations. Indeed, most <<classic>> modulations will be made, directly or indirectly, by means of these chords. We will soon see it.
But first of all, let us review some expressions which will be often used in this chapter:
 * **Initial Key** = scale (key) in which the piece is played <u>before the Modulation.</u>

 * **New (substitute) Key**=new playing scale (key) <u>after Modulation.</u>

 *" **Modulating" Chord** = Chord by which we enter (or go into) the new key.
                In other words, chord allowing the transition to the new playing scale.
                It therefore belongs to the new (substitute) key.
                It will be indicated in red in this chapter.
 We are going, for obvious didactic purposes, to regroup <<classic>> modulations in 3 groups: modulations by means of major, minor and external chords.

I. <u>MAJOR MODULATING CHORDS</u>

It is the most frequent case.
Most guitarists will have already come across it. The modulating chord will be one of the <<pillar chords >> of the substitute key.
It will therefore simply involve entering the new key through of one of its major chords, in this case the chords of harmonic positions I, IV, or V.

*<u>Note:</u>
The change of key will sound much <<smoother>> if the new key is located a fourth (2,5 tones) or a fifth (3,5 tones) higher than the initial one because the chords of these scales are more or less similar.
As we have said before, these chords help identify the major character of a key. They will therefore appear in a way or another (directly or indirectly) during the execution of any modulation of the major scales.

A. <u>MODULATING CHORD V(7)</u>

It is one of the most frequent modulations because, as mentioned earlier on, the V7chord <<dominates>> the key while resolving to the tonic chord I. As a result the modulation is easy to perceive by the ear.

-Example 1: Modulation from the scale of D (initial key) towards the scale of C (new key).

```
       D     Em       A      G
   || / / / /  | / / / /  |
      I (D)  IIm (D)   V (D)  IV (D)
       D     Em       A      G          C
   |  / / / /  | / / / /  | / / / /
                         V(C)       I (C)
```

The Vchord(G) resolves to I (C)

-Example 2: from E to D

```
       E                A                B
   |  / / / /  |  / / / /  |  / / / /  |
      I (E)            IV(E)            V(E)

                D     D7       G      A        D
   | E - A - G | / / / /  | / / / /  | / / / /
      I(E) V(D) IV(D)  I(D)   I7(D)      IV(G)  V(D)     I (D)
```

After the modulation, there is a transition from the V (=A) towards the IV (=G), before playing the tonic chord (I) of the new key.

B. <u>MODULATING CHORD IV</u>

-Example 1: from D to C

```
     Bm          A    B      D - F    C    F
   | / / / /  | / / / /  | / / / / | / / / / |
    IV (D)       V(D)  IV(D)   I(D)  IV(C)  I (C)  IV(C)
      G    F     C
   | / / / /  | / / / /  | . .   . .
    V(C)  IV(C)    I(C)
```

The modulating chord is played after the tonic chord of the initial key.

Example 2: from A to the C

```
   |   A    |    D    |   E    |    D    |    A    |
      I (A)       IV(A)        V(A)       VI(A)       I (A)

     F  -  G  |    C    | . .  . ..
    IV(C)   V(C)       I(C)
```

After modulation, quick transition from IV to V before resolving to the I chord of the new key.

C. <u>MODULATING CHORD I</u>

Example 1: from G to the F

```
‖   G    |     C    |    G    |    D 7   |
   I(G)        IV(G)      I(G)       V(G)
```

```
| G -   F   |   B♭   |    C   | . . . .
  I(G)  I(F)    IV(F)      V(F)
```

Both tonic chords of both keys are played one after the other during the modulation.

Example 2: from F towards C

```
   F            Gm         F   C      C    F
| / / / / | / / / / | / / / / | / / / / |
  I(F)        IIm(F)     I(F) I(C)   I(C) IV(C)
    G      F      C
| / / / / | / / / / | . . . . .
  V(C)   IV(C)  I(C)
```

II. <u>MINOR MODULATING CHORDS</u>

The chords most often involved are the **IIm** and the **VIm**, which will generally be followed by the V7chord (pillar chord).
The IIm chord could, however, sometimes be followed by a I chord instead of a V7.

A. <u>MODULATING CHORD IIm</u>

In many pieces of jazz, this chord will be, during the modulation, incorporated in a II-V-I chord progression type in the new key.
Example 1: from C to F

```
‖ C (M7) | Em (7) | Am (7) | Gm (7) - C7 | F (M7) |
   I(C)      IIIm (C)   VIm (C)   IIm (F)  V7(F)     I(F)
```

Example 2: from C towards B♭

```
‖ Dm (7) - G (7) | C(M7) | Cm (7) - F7 | B♭...
  IIm C    V7(C)    I(C)     IIm(B♭) V7   I(B♭)
```

The last chord of the initial key = the first chord of the new key, here. But note, however, the change of harmonic function.

Example 3: from C towards A♭

```
‖ C (M7) | Bm7♭5) | B♭m (7) | E♭7 | A♭ (M7)...
   I (C)    VIIm♭5 (C)   IIm( A♭)   V7(A♭)   I (A♭)
```

The last chord of the initial key and the first chord of the new key are only a semitone apart.

Example 4: from A towards C

```
‖ A    | D | Dm (7) | C  -  F  | G  -  F   |C.
  I(A)   IV(A)  IIm( c)   I(C)   IV(C)   V(C)   IV(C)   I(C)
```

Here the modulating chord IIm is not incorporated in a II-V-I chord progression type. It is immediately followed by the Chord I of the substitute key.

B. MODULATING CHORD VIm

```
      A       D      E       D      A        D      E
‖ /  /  /  /  | /  /  /  /  | /  /  /  /  | /  /  /  /  |
  I (A)        IV(A)  V(A)       IV(A)  I(A)        I V(A)  V(A)
```

```
    Am              G     F        C
‖ /  /  /  /  | /  /  /  /  | /  /  /  /
  VIm (C)             V(C)  IV(C)       I(C)
```

III.EXTERNAL MODULATING CHORDS

These modulating chords can be external to the initial and / or the new key. It all depends on the sound effects that the guitarist wishes to achieve. One or several external chords can be used, followed generally by a V7 chord, of the new key, which will conclude the modulation as below:
Example: modulation from F towards B♭

```
  F       B♭        C       B♭        F         G   G#
| /  /  /  /  | /  /  /  /  | /  /  /  /  | /  /  /  /  |
  I(F)    IV(F)       V(F)    IV(F)      I(F)
```

```
  F7                B♭
| /  /  /  /  | /  /  /  /  /
  V7(B♭)            I(B♭)
```

*All these <<classic>> modulations that we have just seen will often be performed following a melodic pattern desired by the singer or the guitarist or else in the search for some special melodic effect.

*It therefore becomes apparent , from all the examples mentioned in this chapter, that the guitarist will especially have to concentrate on the last chord before the modulation. All that happens before this chord will depend on the ear or on the inspiration of the guitarist.
Note here, for example, the incorporation of diminished chords in these progressions:

```
Example 1:.. | C | F# dim | D7 | G |....
                            V7(G) I(G)
                    One bar
Example 2:.. | C | C Dim - E♭dim | E7 | A |....
                            V7(A)  I(A)
```

But however, and in spite of all the kinds of modulations seen above, the jazz guitarist, as a good revolutionary, has stepped beyond all these classic notions on the modulation.

He can, indeed, modulate <<from any chord>> of an initial key <<towards any chord>> of a new (substitute) key.

THERE IS TOO MUCH FREEDOM IN THE JAZZ!!!

This is especially true for the instrumental pieces which leave much more freedom of action to the guitarist.

This reality is hence going to prompt us to develop a new working approach of a modulation:

Working method:

1. Make a list of all the comprising chords, of both keys (that of the initial and the new one).
 2. Identify, in the new key, the chords which are common and / or different from those of the initial key.

3. Conceive finally, a modulation pattern (according to the desired sound effect) while taking the following facts into account:
- a) If we want to make the modulation clearly heard, we will << modulate>> preferably by using the chords of the new key which differ from those of the initial one.
- b) But if, on the contrary, a <<soft modulation> is preferred, we are going to modulate by means of the chords of the new key which are common to those of the initial key.

Exemple 1: modulation from the key of C towards the key of G.

Progression in C	Progression in G
(initial key)	(new key)

CM7		Am7	Dm7	G7	CM7 || GM7	Em7	Am7	D7	GM7
I		VIm	IIm	V7	I	I	VIm	IIm	V7	I

Chords of the key of C	Chords of the key of G

CM7 Dm7 Em7 FM7 G7 Am7 Bm7b5	GM7 Am7 Bm7 CM7 D7 Em7 F#m7b5
I IIm IIIm IV7 V7 VIm VIIm	I IIm IIIm IV V7 VIm VIIm

*The chords that are different from those of the initial key are underlined.
- Now, if we want to make <<obvious>> the effect of the modulation we could, for example, play this:

||CM7 | Am 7 | Dm7 | GM7 | Em7 | Am7-D7 | GM7 | ....

Or

||CM7 | Am 7 | Dm7 - G7 | GM7 | Em7 | Am7-D7 | GM7 | .....

- In case a <<soft modulation>> is desired:

Over one bar

| CM7 | Am 7 | Am7 - D7 | GM7 | Em7 | Am7-D7 | GM7 | ....

Or else

| CM7 | Am 7 | Am7 | GM7 | Em7 | Am7-D7 | GM7 | .....

Example 2: Modulation from D towards G.

Chords of the key of D	Chords of the key of G
DM7 Em7 F#m7 GM7 A7 Bm7 C#m7 b5	GM7 Am7 Bm7 CM7 D7 Em7 F#m7 b5

-In an <<emphasized>> modulation we could play:

||DM7 | Bm 7 | Em7 - A7 | D7 |GM7 | Em7 | Am7-D7 |GM7 |
              IIm(D) V7(D)   V7(G)   I (G)   VIm(G)   IIm(G) V7(G)   I....

- <<Smooth>> modulation :

||DM7 | Bm 7 | Em7 - A7 |GM7 | Em7 | Am7-D7 |GM7 |
              IIm (D) V7(D)   I (G)   VIm(G)....

Comments: 1. In case all the chords of both keys are different, the guitarist will have, in order to emphasize on the modulation, a much broader and arbitrary choice of chords.

Example: Modulation from G towards Eb

Chords of the key of G	Chords of the key of Eb
GM7 Am7 Bm7 CM7 D7 Em7 F#m7 b5	EbM7 Fm7 G m7 G#M7 A#7 Cm7 Dm7 b5
I IIm IIIm IV V7 VIm VIIm	I IIm IIIm IV V7 VIm VIIm

||GM7 | Em7 | Am7-D7 |GM7 | Fm7 - A#7 | Eb7 |.
    I(G)   VI (G)   IIm(G) V7(G)   I(G)   IIm(Eb) V7(Eb) I(Eb)

2.<<Smooth>> modulations will be most probably better achieved from a given initial key towards a new key located at either a tone, or 2,5 tones or else 3,5 tones, higher or lower, because of the existence of at least one common chord.

*Some composers will pursue even further their search for <<sound effects of embellishment >> by creating an << END OF PIECE MODULATION>> as below:

52

Example 1: music piece in A, ending in F.

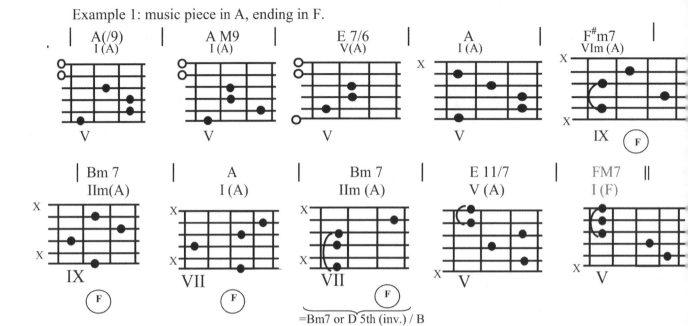

All the chords marked with an (F) are preferably played in finger picking

Example 2: Piece in E, ending in A

| C#m | A | G#m | G#m | A - B | E 9 |
| VIm (E) | IV(E) | IIIm (E) | IIIm (E) | IV(E) V(E) | V(A) |

Jimi Hendrix; performing live onstage, playing black
Fender Stratocaster guitar at K.B. Hallen

CHAP . III <<EXTERNAL>> CHORDS (TO A GIVEN KEY).

These are chords whose roots are notes that do not belong to the key in which the piece is played, without any Modulation* or Chord Substitution * occuring.

Indeed, besides the chords mentioned earlier in page 92 volume1: IImaj (or II7), IIImaj (or III7), VI maj (or VI7) and VIImin, as well as «altered chords», which are non «diatonic» in a key (and because of that, are also external to the key) but still «playable» to get a desired effect, the guitarist could, in certain cases (rather frequent), play a chord whose root note is completely «external» to the key.

One of the most used chords is the **VII^{b}maj** chord.

Example 1 : in the key of C

I	VII^{b}maj	VI (m)	VII^b maj	I
C	B^b	Am	B^b	C

‖ / / / / │ / / / / │ / / / / │ / / / / │ / / / /

(H)　　　　　(B)　　　　(B)　　　　(B)　　　　(H)

*Modulation: Change of key occuring during the execution of a music piece, over a few bars or the rest of the piece.
*Chord Substitution : SEE CHAPTER ON THIS SUBJECT.

Example 2: still in C

I	VII^{b}maj	VI (maj)	V	V7
C	B^b maj	A	G	G7

‖ / / / / │ / / / / │ / / / / │ / / / / │ / / / / │

(GB)　　　　(GB)　　　　(GB)　　　　(H)　　　(H)

I
C

│ / / / / │ . . . . .

(H)

Example 3: in C

I	VII^{b}maj	VI(m)	V	IV	I
C	B^{b}maj	Am	G	F	C

‖ / / / / │ / / / / │ / / / / │ . . . .

55

Example 4: In the key of F

I	V	IV	VII^{b}maj
F	C	B^b	E^b

‖ / / / / | / / / / | / / / / | / / / / |

(GB)or(PH)	(B)	(GB)	(B)
V	I		
C	F		

| / / / / | / / / / | . . . .

(B)   (PH)

Remark: This 4ᵗʰ example gives the guitarist the rare opportunity to create what we would call an<<u>artificial resolution</u>>, during the transition from the IVchord towards the VII^b.
Indeed, the interval of tones between the IV and VII^b chords is the same as that of the V7 and I chords, during a natural resolution, which is 2,5 tones (see page1).
This will then allow us to play a IV7 on a part of the IV chord bar, before playing the VII^b like this:

artificial resolution

I	V	IV	IV7	VII^{b}maj
F	C	B^b	B^{b}7	E^b

‖ / / / / | / / / / | / / / / | / / / / |

V	I
C	F

| / / / / | / / / / | . . . .

* The IV7 chord played in that way also becomes external to the key, but with a diatonic root note.
- The **III^{b}maj** chord is also used in some other harmonic situations.

Example in A:

I	III^{b}maj	IV	III^{b}maj	I
A	C	D	C	A

‖ / / / / | / / / / | . . . .

(B)   (B)   (B)   (B)   (B)

- The **VI^b maj** chord will be played in a rather BLUES ROCK context as in the following example in E: <<Hey Jo>> (Jimmy Hendricks).

I	I	VI^{b}maj	III^{b}maj	VII^{b}maj	IV	I
E	E	C	G	D	A	E

‖ / / / / | / / / / | / / / / | / / / / | / / / / | . . . .

(GB)   (GB)   (B)   (GB)   (B)   (GB)   (GB)

We will end this chapter with quite an interesting example on the use of external chords taken from the famous song <<Hello>> by Lionel Richie.

Here the **VI maj** chord is intercalated during the transition from the IVchord towards the II chord as this:

```
   VIm            V6            IV              VImaj           IIm
   Am             G6            FM7             A               Dm
| /   /   /   / | /   /   /   / | /   /   /   / | /   /   /   / | /   /   /   / |
   V              I             IV              VIIᵇ maj        IIImaj
   G              C             F               Bᵇ              E
| /   /   /   / | /   /   /   / | /   /   /   / | /   /   /   / | /   /   /   / |

   VIm
   Am
| /   /   /   / | . . . .
```

This produces a nice << resolution sound effect >> ,very interesting (following the example of the resolution of the V7chord to the I chord) while resolving to a minor chord (IIm).

Indeed the two chords (IVand II) are separated by an interval of 2,5 tones, fulfiling the usual requirement for a resolution.

Notice also, in the meanwhile, the presence of some other external chords as the VII ^{b} maj and the IIImaj, in the chord progression.

But the guitarist, here, was even much more subtle by ending the song with an external chord: the same A major= VI major (see the complete chord progression of the song).

In conclusion, and as it is obvious from now on, these chords, while being << external >> to a given key, can really be played there and bring new colours.

THEY ARE THEREFORE EXTERNAL BUT WITHOUT SOUNDING OUT OF TUNE!!!

The piece involved will generally have a <<Blues - Rock>> sound.

CHAP. IV. <u>POLYTONAL CHORDS</u>

We could not end our study on chords in this work, without mentioning the polytonal chords, which are of very recent use in contemporary modern music.

Literally, a polytonal chord is a chord belonging to more than one key (scale) at the same time. There are, in practice, two kinds of polytonal chords:

1st Kind: These are chords containing two other « implied » chords (triads). It simply means that with the notes composing these chords, we can form two other different chords, which, played at the same time, will give the sound of this initial chord.

These types of polytonals chords are often extended chords of more than 4 notes.

Example: C 9

It is made up of the following notes:

C	E	G	B^b	D
1	3	5	7	9

You will notice that, in fact, this chord could be analysed as the superimposing of the two following triads:

C major (C, E, G) and the **G minor** (G, B^b, D).

The rhythm guitarist could therefore, for example, play the C major chord while the lead guitarist will play the G minor, to reconstruct the sound of the **C 9** chord.

Same reasoning for this second example: **C11**

C 11 = C	E	B	B^b	D	F
1	3	5	7	9	11

It will be analysed as **a Cmajor** (C,E, G) plus a **B^b major** (B^b, D, F).

2ⁿᵈ **_kind:_** These are chords that often have the form of **extended chords** but **without the third note**.

Therefore, if you see a chord without third, try, having excluded other possibilities, to analyse it as a polytonal chord. Because the third, as stipulated in this work, is the characteristic note of most chords. It cannot miss, unless dealing with a **suspended fourth** chord (Sus 4) or **second**, etc …

In other words, these chords will have **the appearance of an extended chord or of an altered chord in "Root position" but of which some notes will be omitted**. The notes which will be most often left out, if the chord is analysed in that way, will be the **third** (as said earlier on) and the **fifth**.

Their composition is simple. They are 4 sounds chords (meaning, 4 different notes) made of a **triad** or a simple chord (major, minor, augmented or diminished) associated with a **bass note** which is not the normal root note of that chord (or triad).

This bass note will be 1. Either a note belonging to the key of the triad without however being part of the triad itself **(tonal bass note)**.

           2. Or a note taken outside the key of the triad **(altered or non-tonal bass note)**.

It will therefore be simply a question of playing **a simple triad on a bass note belonging or not to its key**.

This unusual composition give them a particular harmonic characteristic which is that of being **"bi-tonal"** (especially when the bass note is not tonal).

The first key is that of the triad and the second is that of the bass note.

These chords will be named, as a result, with **2 names separated by a slash**, or written in the form of a **fraction**: the first name (or numerator) represents the triad (or chord) while the second (or the denominator) represents the bass note.

For example: **C/D** or $\frac{C}{D}$ will mean that the **triad of C** with a **bass note D** is played.

The analysis of these chords will be made in a very simple way: it will be enough to subtract the bass note to find the triad (or chord) of origin, to which the bass note was associated.

This second kind of polytonal chords is more and more used in pop music and others, allowing the guitarist to create new tones, for example by forming chromatic bass line motions thus getting some very interesting ascending or descending effects, as we will see an example in the **chapter on chord substitutions**.

They have, moreover, a clear and simple, pure sound, highlighting the 2 keys, that of the triad and of the bass note.

Here are some examples in **C** and **other keys** :

I. Bass note (C) with **major triad** (or chord):

* **D/C:**

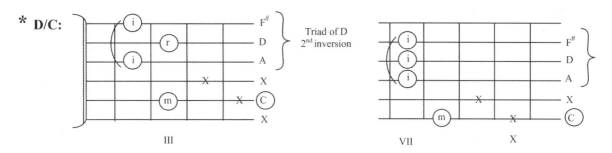

- Note that the bass note **C**, is the **7ᵗʰ** note in the scale of **D** As a result, the chord could be considered as well to be an « opened » **D7** chord, with the **7ᵗʰ** note in the bass (Harmonic on the left and Grand harmonic on the right).

* **G/C:**

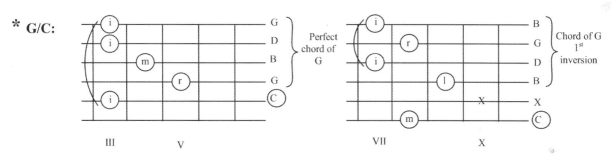

- If we consider the note **C** to be the root note of this chord, you will notice that it will give a **C M9 chord without third**. (Barré on the left and Grand barré on the right).

* **Bᵇ/C**

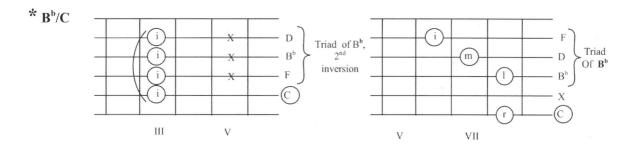

- Similarly to the previous chord, if one thinks of the note C as the root note of the chord, we will have a **C11 chord without third, nor fifth**. What is, as we have seen, equivalent to the **C9 sus 4 chord** (Barré on the left and Grand barré on the right).

II. Bass note with **minor triad** (or chord):

* **Cm/F =** basse note **F** with triad of **C minor**

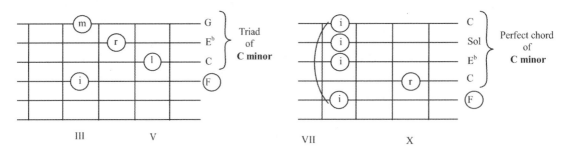

- If the bass note is considered as the root note, the chord would be a **F9 without a third** (Small barré on the left and Barré on the right).

* **Mim/F** – Bass note **F** with triad of E **minor**

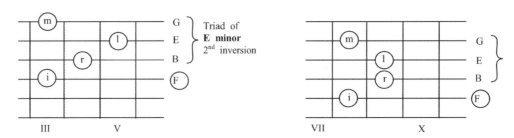

- It could give a **FM9^{b}5 chord without a third** if the note F is considered as the root (Small barré on the left and Barré on the right).
But we could however apply here a different reasoning: the chord could also be thought as a **6th** chord of harmonic form (Small harmonic on the left and Harmonic on the right) whose root has been lowered by a tone to give a **7th** note, hence giving an inversion of the **G7/6** chord, with the note **7 (F)** in the bass, as seen before (Small harmonic on the left and Harmonic on the right).

* **Cm/B** – Bass note **B** with triad of **Cminor**.

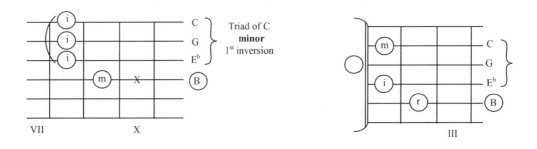

- If we consider the bass note **B** as the **M7** note of the scale of **C**, the chord would be like a **CmM7** with the note **M7** (B) in the bass.

Bob Marley performing live on stage, playing guitar

Important remark:

The notation, in fraction, peculiar to polytonal chords has been recently widely used by several authors to describe chord inversions.

That use has become so extensive that it has almost supplanted this concept of chord inversions in most of <<song books>> on the market.

The main purpose in the concept is to be able to indicate accurately the bass note (the lowest note) played in the inversion in question and which we want to highlight.

As an example we will take two simple chord progressions from the repertoire of the legendary Bob Marley:

1. <<No woman no cry>>, written by Vincent Ford (sung and made popular by Bob Marley)

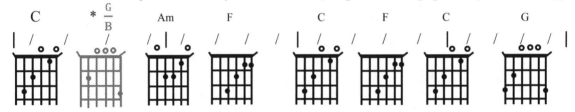

*The chord G/B is nothing else than the inversion of the chord G (neck end Grand Harmonic), which has the note B as bass note.

2. <<Turn your ligths down low>>, lyrics and music by Bob Marley

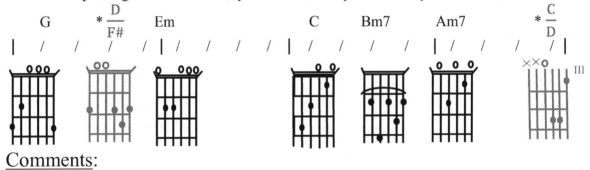

Comments:

1. The chord D/F$^{\#}$ is simply the basic chord D played with its third (F$^{\#}$) on the 6th string, note that we wanted to highlight on the bass line.

2. Only the chord C/D is a true polytonal chord according to the descriptions seen before.

In modern music, the concept of polytonal chords, as seen earlier, has been broadened by incorporating in the list two new (unusual) forms of polytonal chords.

These new forms will often appear on scores initially written for piano but played on the guitar. A nice illustration is given in the music of Lionel Richie (and many other musicians) which we are going to try to analyze here, by means of some examples.

A. Polytonals chords built with the aid of «particular» triads described in the chapter III section C.2 of the volume 1 (from page 62 up to page 72).

The most used particular triads will be the **sus2, 3rd, 5th** and **sus4.**

Examples:
1.With a triad of 3rd:

* **G^3 /C** = triad of G3rd with a bass note in C

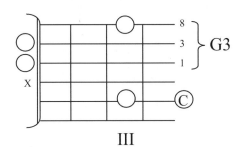

III

<<Ballerina Girl>> by Lionel Richie (key of C):

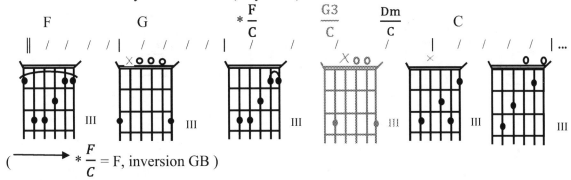

(———→ * $\frac{F}{C}$ = F, inversion GB)

*** G^3 / F** = Triad of G3rd with a bass note in F.

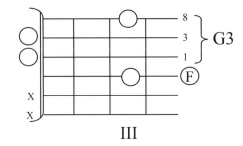

III

<<Soon as I get home>> by Kenneth EDMONDS <<Baby Face>> (Key of G)

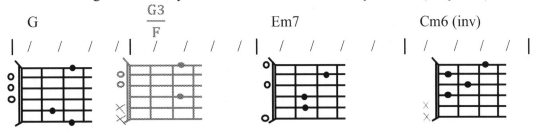

2. <u>With a triad of 5th</u> :

*G ^{5}/ B = triad of G5^e with a bass note in B.

- 1st form:

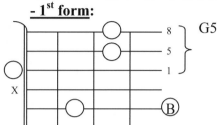

<< Dancing on the ceiling >> by L. Richie : key of C

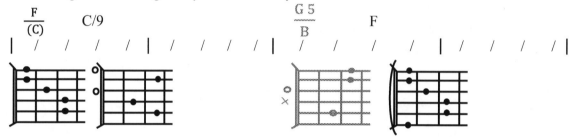

- 2nd form:

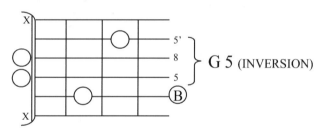

<<You are>> by L. RICHIE: in C (capo* on the 1st fret)

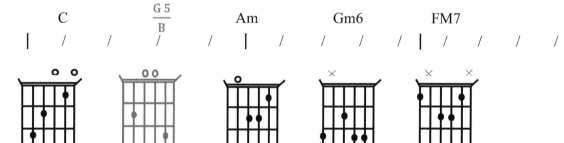

*C^5 / E = triad of C^5 with a bass note in E.

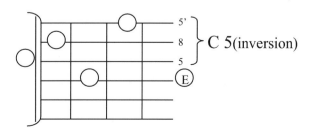

<<Truly>> by L. RICHIE: in C (capo* on the 1st fret)

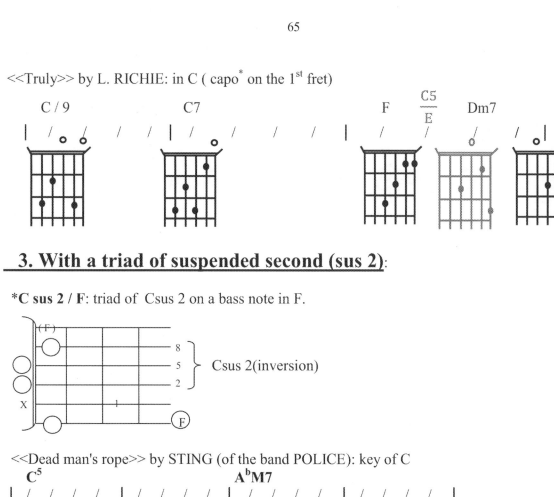

C / 9   C7   F $\frac{C5}{E}$ Dm7

3. With a triad of suspended second (sus 2):

*C sus 2 / F: triad of Csus 2 on a bass note in F.

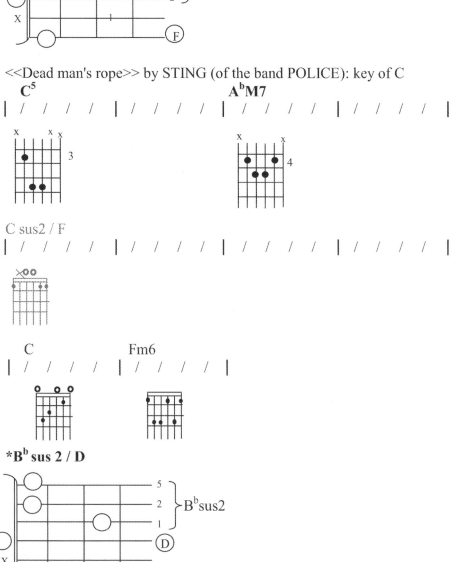

<<Dead man's rope>> by STING (of the band POLICE): key of C

C⁵   AᵇM7

C sus2 / F

C   Fm6

*Bᵇ sus 2 / D

<<Why does it hurt so bad>>, by K. EDMONDS <<Baby Face>> ,in B^b

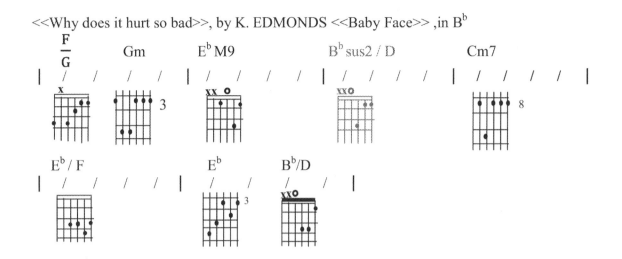

$\dfrac{F}{G}$ Gm   E^b M9   B^b sus2 / D   Cm7

E^b / F   E^b B^b/D

4. With a triad of suspended fourth(sus 4):

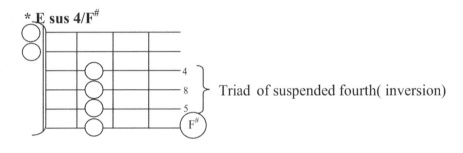

* E sus 4/F$^\#$

Triad of suspended fourth(inversion)

<<change the world>> by W. KIRK PATRICK, G.KENNEDY and T. SIMS in E

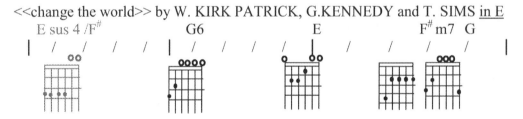

E sus 4 /F$^\#$ G6   E   F$^\#$m7   G

In practice, any kind of triads can be used in the construction of polytonal Chords.

B. Polytonal chords constructed not with the aid of a triad but of an <<entire>> chord (either fundamental or extended chord or else others) linked to a bass note.

The purpose here is, very clearly, to highlight a particular note which must be played on one of the bass strings to give the desired sound effect.

The resulting chord could, moreover, have a double name. In other words, if we wish to ignore that << desired sound effect>>, the chord could very well be named differently, that is to say not like a polytonal chord.

We will see it in the examples below:

1. **FM7 / G**

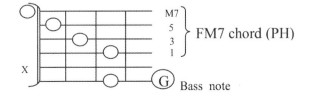

FM7 chord (PH)

Bass note

The << desired effect>> here , is to have the note G on the 6th string .However the chord could just as well be considered as a FM9 (with the note 9 on the bass string or , even as a G13 sus 4 (Root position).

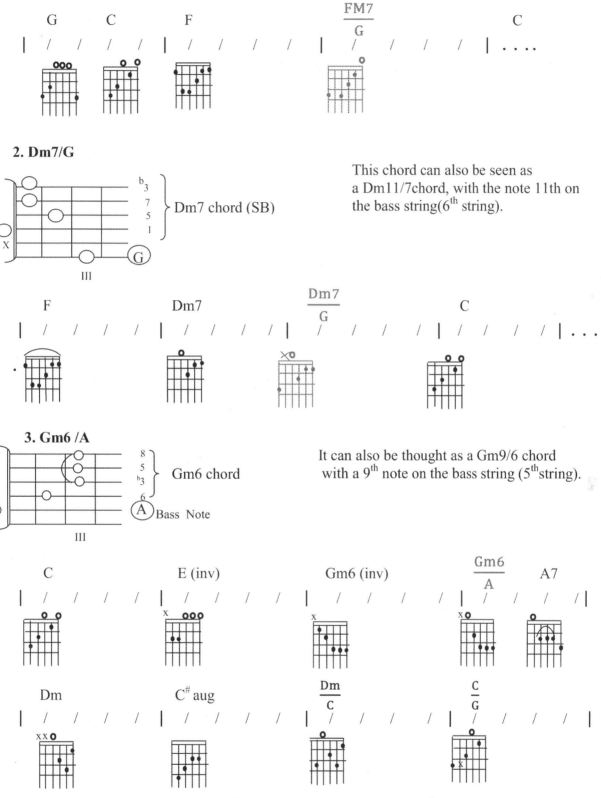

2. Dm7/G

Dm7 chord (SB)

This chord can also be seen as a Dm11/7chord, with the note 11th on the bass string(6th string).

3. Gm6 /A

Gm6 chord

It can also be thought as a Gm9/6 chord with a 9th note on the bass string (5thstring).

Note the descending chromatic melodic line motion created on the 5th string!!!

4. Cdim / G

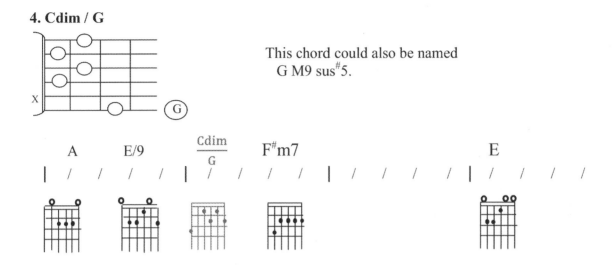

This chord could also be named
G M9 sus#5.

All the above examples lead us to agree that, eventually, any kind of chord can be linked to a bass note to form a polytonal chord.

In conclusion, polytonal chords are in reality nothing else than some kinds of <<artificial inversions>> (meaning non diatonic), constructed in the same purpose as the <<natural inversions>> (of the diatonic scale) which is, to create a particular sound effect or just to<< match>> the melody line.

Recording artist **Kenneth Brian 'Babyface' Edmonds** performs at the Fulfillment Fund 'Songs Of Our Lives' Benefit Concert at the Geffen Playhouse on May 22, 2012 in Los Angeles, California

CHAP.V. <u>SYNONYMOUS CHORDS</u>

Synonymous Chords are chords (2 chords or more) which are made up of the same notes, but have different names however.

These identical notes could be arranged in a different order in each of the concerned chords.

These chords will not always have the same notes straightaway. It will be needed (in the majority of the cases) in order to achieve that, to subtract a note which will be called in this work " **differential note** ", from one of the chords.

It is the note that gives the difference of names between the 2 chords and, without which the 2 chords will be identical.

We point out here that it would be possible, sometimes, to have up to two differential notes.

The most known «differential note» is the **root note(1)** (of the initial chord), followed by the **fifth (5)**. We said previously that the root note **(1)** and the fifth **(5)** were not necessary notes in a chord.

This phenomenon is due to the fact that the musician, having only 12 different notes in every scale (12 chromatic notes) to construct a great number of chords, can only built a limited number chord without repeating any notes.

The simplest example is that of **relative chords** (relative majors or minors):

- *Eg. 1:* **Am7** without root is synonymous with **Cmaj** (Am7 is the relative minor chord of C major).

$$\begin{array}{cccc} 1 & 3 & 5 & 7 \end{array}$$

Let us analyse their composition: -A**m7**:   A / C / E / G

$$\begin{array}{ccc} 1 & 3 & 5 \end{array}$$

- **C Maj:** X / C / E / G

* Note: the note **A** is the differential note here. It is the note to be subtracted!

In practice, in a music piece, both chords could therefore be interchangeable without any problem meaning, without modification of the harmony of the group.

In case however **the root note of the initial chord is the differential note**, it will have to be played either by the bassist, or by the lead guitarist or else the keyboard player, to maintain the "cadence" of the song. The same technique is to be applied if there is no differential note at all.

Eg. 2: **C6** without fifth **(5)** = **A minor**

Compositions : **C 6** : $\overset{1}{C}$ / $\overset{3}{E}$ / $\overset{5}{\cancel{G}}$ / $\overset{6}{A}$

A m : $\overset{1}{A}$ / $\overset{3}{C}$ / $\overset{5}{E}$

Differential note = G

This notion, as one can notice, is going to enrich the harmonic vocabulary of the rhythm guitarist and is, as a result, going to multiply his possibilities of choice of chords by two (at least).

Important remark: there will be, on the other hand, possibility of rendering those chords identical, without leaving out any note of the first chord, by adding the differential note to the second chord:

- From example N°1:

Am 7 (without root) = C **major**. Differential note =**A**

Now, C **major** + A = C / E / G /A
$$= \textbf{C 6}$$
$$= \textbf{Am7} \ (A \ /C \ / E \ / G)$$

We are going to end this chapter by listing the most known cases in tables which will make them easier to assimilate.

Key:
- 1 = without root
- 5 = without fifth
- 1,-5 = without root, nor fifth
- **H** = harmonic, **GH** = Grand Harmonic, **SH** = Small Harmonic
- **B** = Barré, **GB** = Grand barré, **SB** = Small barré
- 2T = 2 tones higher, 2T = 2 tones lower

* The **«Preferred shapes»** of chords are shapes for which, these resemblances are straightaway visible on the keyboard.
* To better put these notions into practice, refer to intervals seen in page 82 (volume 1).

MAJOR CHORDS

INITIAL CHORD			SYNONYMOUS CHORD		
Chords	**Preferential Shapes**	Differential Note(s)	**Synonymous Chord(s)**	**Preferential Shapes**	**Number of tones in comparison with the initial chord**
6 : - 0	B & GB	NONE	**Minor 7**	SH, H	1,5 tone ↘
- 5	ALL	5	**Minor**	ALL	1,5 tone ↘
M7 : - 1	H, GH and SH	1	**Minor**	SH, H, triad	2 tones ↗
	B & GB	1	**6th without fifth (5)**	SH, H	3,5 T ↗ ou 2,5 ↘
M6 : - 1	B, GB	1	**9/6 without fifth (5)**	SH, H	3,5 T ↗ ou 2,5 T ↘
- 1, - 5	⌠ H, SH	1 & 5	**Sus 4** ⟶	SH, triad	2T ↗
	⌡ H ⟶		**2nd chord** ⟶	B	1,5 T ↘
9/6 : - 1	H, GH	1	**m 11/7 without 5**	SB & B	2T ↗
			7 sus 4	B & GB	1,5 T ↗
M9 : - 1	B & GB	1	**m 7**	SB & B	2T ↗
			6th chord	SB & B	3,5T ↗ ou 2,5T ↘
M7#11 : - 1 & -5	H & GH	1	**m/9 chord**	ALL	2T ↗
	B & GB	1	**2nd chord**	ALL	2T ↗
M6/9 : - 1	GH	1	**m 11/7**	B	2T ↗
	B & GB	1 & 5	**7 sus 4**	SB + B	2T ↗
M6#11 : - 1, -5	B & GB	1 & 5	**m 11/7 without 5**	SB & B	3T ↗
M 13#11: -1, -5	H & GH	1 & 5	**m 11/7 (with 5)**	B & GB	2T ↗

MINOR CHORDS

INITIAL CHORD			SYNONYMOUS CHORD		
Chords	**Preferential Shape(s)**	Differential Note(s)	**Synonymous Chord(s)**	**Preferential Shape(s)**	**Number of tones in comparison with the initial chord**
m 6 : - 5	H, SH	5	- m^{b}5 ⟶	B, SB ⟶	1,5 tones ↘
			- 7th without root ▸	SH, B ⟶	2,5 tones ↗
- 0	H	NONE	**9** without root	SH	2,5 tones ↗
m7 : - 1	B, GB	⋮	**Major chord**	H, GH(1thinv.)	1,5 tones ↗
- 0	H, SH	NONE	**7 sus 4** (without 1)	GB, B	2,5T ↗
	B, GB	NONE	**6th chord**	H, GH (top note = 6)	1,5T ↗
m7^{b}5 : 0	H & GH	NONE	**m 6 chord**	B, SB	1,5, T ↗
- 1	B, GB, SB	⋮	**Minor chord**	H, GH, SH(1st inv.) SH, H	1,5 T ↗
			6th chord(witout 5)		3 T ↗
m7^{b}5^{b}6 : - 1	B & GB	⋮	**6/9 chord** (without5)	SH, H	3T ↗
m9 : - 1	ALL	⋮	**7 M**	ALL	1,5T ↗
m 11/7 : - 1	H & GH	⋮	**2nd chord**	SB, B	1,5T ↗
m 11^{b}5 : - 1	H, GH	⋮	**6M chord**(without 5)	SH, H	3T ↗
	B, GB, SB	⋮	**m/9 chord**	H, GH, SH	1,5T ↗
m 7^b 6/11 : - 5	B & GB	5	**m 11/7**	SB & B	2,5T ↗
- 1, -5	B, GB	1, 5	**7 sus 4 chord**	B, GB	1 T ↘
m 11/7/6 : - 5	B, GB	5	**11/7 chord**	SB, B	2,5T ↗

DOMINANT CHORDS

	INITIAL CHORD			SYNONYMOUS CHORD	
Chords	**Preferential Shapes**	**Differential Note(s)**	**Synonymous Chord(s)**	**Preferential Shapes**	**Number of tones in comparison with the initial chord**
7 : - 1	B, GB	¦	**m 6** (without 5)	SH, H	2,5 Tones ↘
7/6 : - 1	B, GB	¦	**m 9/6** (without 5)	SH, H	2,5 Tones ↘
9 : - 1	H, GH	¦	**m7ᵇ5**	SB, B	2T ↗
	B, GB	¦	**m 6**	SH, H	2,5T ↘
13 : - 1	GB	¦	**m 9/6** (with 5)	H	2,5, T ↘
7 sus 4 : - 1	B, GB	¦	**m 7** (without 5)	SH, H	2,5T ↘
- 0	B, GB	NONE	**m 11/7** (without 5)	SB, B	2,5T ↘
9 sus 4 : - 1	B, GB	¦	**m 7** (with 5)	SH, H	2,5T ↘
	GB	¦	**6ᵗʰ** (with 5)	SB	1 T ↘
13 sus 4 : - 1	B, GB	¦	**M7**	B, SB	1T ↘
7ᵇ5 : - 0	B, GB	NONE	**7ᵇ5** ⟶	B, GB	3T ↗
- 1	B, GB	¦	**7ᵗʰ Chord** (without 5)	SH, H	3T ↗
9ᵇ5 : - 0	B, GB (invers)	NONE	**9 #5**	H, GH	1T ↗
- 1	H, GH	¦	**7 #5**	SH, H	3T ↗
13ᵇ5 : - 1	B, GB	¦	**7#5#9**	B, GB	3T ↗
9#5 : - 1	H, GH	¦	**7ᵇ5**	SB, B	2T ↗
7#5#9 : - 1	H, GB	¦	**13** (without 1)	SH, H	3T ↗
7ᵇ9 : - 1	H, GH	¦	**Diminished chord**	SB, B	2T ↗
7ᵇ5#9 : - 1	B, GB	¦	**7/6** (without 5)	GB, B	3T ↗
7ᵇ5ᵇ9#9 : - 1	H, GH	¦	**7/6** (with 5)	GB, B	3T ↗

7#5b9#9 : - 1	B, GB	ꜜ	13 (without 1)	B, GB	3T ↗

Remark: you will surely have noticed that the chord 7b5 is exactly the same as the one built 3 tones higher.
It simply shows that it repeats itself every 7 frets (3 tones).

Keith Richards performing live onstage with the Rolling Stones,
playing Gibson ES-355 guitar with Bigsby vibrato

CHAP.VI. <u>CHORD SUBSTITUTION</u>

Beyond any theoretical considerations, the notion of chord substitution has the only and simple purpose of bringing some variation or harmonic modification in a sequence of chord or a given chord progression.

As a result,of course,that will allow the introduction of new « nuances » or desired sound effects or else the bringing-in of new colours or new harmonic ideas to embelish chord sequences considered too simple or monotonous.

Some rhythm guitarists have even so much mastered the art of chord substitution that they use it as a means of « improvisation », following the example of the lead guitarist (soloist).

In a simple and practical way, we will say that the substitution of chord is only made in 2 ways: vertically and horizontally.

A. IN A VERTICAL WAY

It simply consists in changing(extending,altering or replacing) existing chord.
We will maintain, in most cases, the harmonic positions and functions of these existing chords.
What will happen,in practical terms, is that the guitarist will change some chords of the progression by playing their extended forms or their altered forms, without changing their harmonic positions however or by simply replacing them with their synonymous or relative chords (or others).
Let us note that in the latter case the harmonic functions and positions will change automatically.

Moreover, only the harmonic function will change if we desire, for example, to transform momentarily a given « initial chord » into a « **passing chord**». It will then be necessary to take into account the interval of tones, between that initial (original) chord and the modified (substutition) chord.

B. IN A HORIZONTAL WAY

It consists in adding one or more additional chords to a given chord progression.
It will be a question of using the interval of **tones** and the available **beats** (of a bar) between the roots of two adjacent chords of a progression, in order to add to it (to insert) one or several extra chords, which are going to link up both pre-existing chords.

We therefore mainly take into account,here, the intervals between the roots of the existing chords, for the choice the substitution chords, while the number of chords to be inserted will depend on the available number of **"beats"** in the bar.

A. VERTICAL SUBSTITUTIONS

Three possibilities present themselves to the guitarist:

1. Simple **"replacement"** of existing chords

2. Use of the **extended forms** of existing chords (or even simpler chords)

3. **Chromatic alterations** of existing chords

I. SIMPLE REPLACEMENTS:

The existing chord(original chord) is replaced with its **synonym** or its **relative chord** or else with **another form**(or shape) of the same chord (for example: a harmonic for a barré or a barré for an inversion, etc…), with the intention of bringing new colours in the played piece.

Example 1: Substitution by a relative chord

It will be made by completely substituting the existing **major chord** by its **primary relative minor** (1,5 tone) or by its **secondary relative minor** (2 tones) or conversely!

a) Substitution of a **major chord** by its **relative minor**:

- **Original progression** (chords played at the end of the neck) :

```
      G              C      D        G
|  /  /   /   /  |  /  /   /   /  |  /  /   /   /  |
  (GH)           (H)   (PB)
```

- **Substitution**: The chord **G** is completely replaced with its relative minor which is **Em** (or **Em 7**)

```
   Em(7)            C      D       G
|  /  /   /   /  |  /  /   /   /  |  /  /   /   /  |
  (GB)
```

b) Substitution of a **major chord** by its **secondary relative minor**

- **Original progression** (at the end of the neck) :

```
    C      A7        Dm   G7        C
|  /  /  /  /  |  /  /  /  /  |  /  /  /  /  |
  (H)    (B)      (SB) (GH)      (H)
```

- **Substitution**: C is replaced with its secondary relative minor which is **Em**(or **Em7**)

```
  Em(7)  A7         Dm   G7        CM7
|  /  /  /  /  |  /  /  /  /  |  /  /  /  /  |
  (GB)
```

c) Substitution of a **minor chord** by its **relative major**:

- **Original progression** :

```
    C      Am        Dm   G7        C
|  /  /  /  /  |  /  /  /  /  |  /  /  /  /  |
  (H)    (B)      (SB) (GH)      (H)
```

- **Substitution** : the chords **Am** and **Dm** are replaced with their respective relative major chords, **C** and **F**.

```
    C                F    G7        CM7
|  /  /  /  /  |  /  /  /  /  |  /  /  /  /  |
  (H)             (GB) (GH)      (H)
```

Example 2: Substitution by another form(shape) of the same chord

- **Original progression :**

```
     C                    F     Dm        G7              C
|  /   /   /   /  |   /   /   /   /  |   /   /   /   /  |   /   /   /   /  |
   (H)                 (GB)  (SB)       (GH)              (H)
```

- **Substitution** : the chords **Dm**, **G** and **C** are replaced with some other forms.

```
     C                    F     Dm        G7              C
|  /   /   /   /  |   /   /   /   /  |   /   /   /   /  |   /   /   /   /  |
                              (B)        (GB)             (B)
```

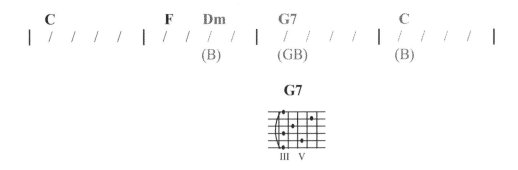

G7

III   V

Example 3: Substitution by a chord of the same name but of a different harmonic function:

We have said at the beginning of the second part of this work that the chords of harmonic positions **II**, **III** and **VI** are naturally minor but could, in certain cases, become major.

These chords (II, III, and VI), as we also said, could even become seventh chords (**7**).
We could therefore use these characteristics in chord substitution as in the example below

- Original progression :

```
        C    Am        Dm   G7        C
   |  /  /  /  /  |  /  /  /  /  |  /  /  /  /  |
      (H)  (B)       (SB) (GH)      (H)
```

- Substitution :

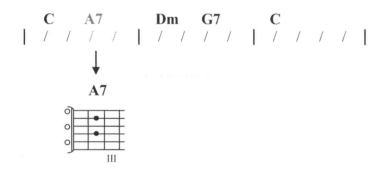

```
        C    A7        Dm   G7        C
   |  /  /  /  /  |  /  /  /  /  |  /  /  /  /  |
             ↓
            A7
```

II. USE Of EXTENDED CHORDS (or simplified, depending on circumstances)

Extended chords will generally be used with the intention of « embellishing » or "enriching" a chord progression.

It will be necessary, by so doing, to give a particular attention to the top and bottom notes, in order to get the desired sound effect.

There are, however, particular situations where their use is strongly requested, notably when 2 chords (often major) are separated by an **interval of a fourth**.

It is appropriate here to state the following general rule:

« Any chord can be transformed into a dominant 7th chord if the following chord is constructed a **fourth** higher » (= resolution).

Two situations are generally encountered:

1. Starting chord= **I** (harmonic position).
   Following chord = **IV**

The original chord **I**, will therefore become a seventh chord (**I7**) thus creating a temporary change of its harmonic function.

This **I7** chord is, here, a **«passing chord»** and, as one can notice, external* to the key. It is one of the simplest examples of substitution.

*External chords, see chapter 3.

Example (in the key of C major):

- Original progression :

```
    C                F                G
|  /   /   /   /  |  /   /   /   /  |  /   /   /   /  |
    I                IV               V
```

- Substitution :

```
    C    C7          F                G
|  /   /   /   /  |  /   /   /   /  |  /   /   /   /  |
    I                IV
```

Comments:

1. The original chord **C** (**I**) is not entirely replaced.
   It is played over 2 beats of the bar and the **I7** chord on the rest of the bar beats.

2. If we want to highlight the note 7 of the chord **I**, we could also use the techniue of simple replacement, as below, putting the note 7 on the bottom string.

Original progression :

```
      C        C7           F
|   /   /   /   /   |   /   /   /   /   |
    (H)      (H)         (SH)
```

- **Substitution :**

```
      C        C7           F
|   /   /   /   /   |   /   /   /   /   |
    (H)      (B)         (SH)
```

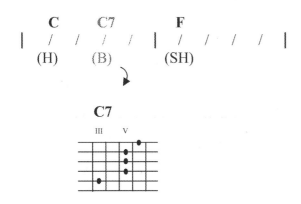

C7

2. Starting chord= **V**
   Following chord = **I**

The **V**chord will become **V7** which is its natural extension, giving therefore
a natural resolution of the **V7** to the **I**.

__Example (in the key of C):__

- **Original progression :**

```
    G              C
|  /  /  /  /   |  /  /  /  /   |
```

- **Substitution**

```
   G7              C
|  /  /  /  /   |  /  /  /  /   |
```

Note that:

a) The substitution can be made straight away on the 1st beat of the bar in this case (the substitution chord is not a passing chord).

b) The **seventh chord** thus formed can, as said earlier on, be substituted in its turn by one or another of its extensions to get any desired sound effect.

But that is not all.
Extended chords can also be used to **"soften** or **"disguise"** the sound of a major, minor or dominant seventh chord.
In this respect, a special mention will be made for the **dominant chords** (harmonic position **V**) which will be "extended" in order either to **"accentuate** or **"soften" the resolution effect.**

For example, it is possible to substitute **the seventh chord** (**7**), in position **V**, for **the eleventh chord** (or **9 sus 4**) which will have the same harmonic function but, on the contrary, have a more « disguised » sound , as below:

- Original progression: V→ I

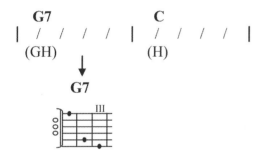

- Substitution :

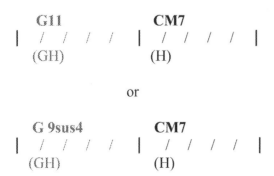

Comments:

1. While playing these two different progressions, you will have noticed that even though both the **G7** and **G11** (or **9 sus 4**) chords are dissonant and therefore need to resolve to **C maj**, the **11**[th] chord is however much less dissonant and has, so, less need to resolve to **C** (disguised effect!).

2. Note also that if the resolution effect is simply <u>not wanted</u>, the seventh chord will be, on the contrary, bluntly brought back (simplified) into a fundamental major chord.
Indeed, the harmonic variation of a progression can be achieved by merely changing only one note in a chord.

3. If the resolution effect is, on the contrary,<u>wanted</u>, there is also a form of substitution which consists in preparing the coming of the **V7** chord by a **9 sus 4** or **11**[th] chord played on the 2 first beats of its bar, as follows:

Example 1:

- Original progression :

```
     C      C7          F             G7              C
 |  /  /  /  /  |  /  /  /  /  |  /  /  /  /  |  /  /  /  /  |
    (H)   (H)      (SH)          (GH)           (H)
```

- Substitution:

```
 | C  /  C7  /  |  F  /  /  /  | G 9 sus 4  /  G7  /  |  C M7  /  /  /  |
```

Exemple 2 :

- Original progression :

```
   C       C7          F           G7              C
|  /   /   /   /   |   /   /   /   /   |   /   /   /   /   |   /   /   /   /   |
  (H)     (H)        (SH)          (GB)            (B)
```

- Substitution:

```
   C       C7          F             G 11   G7      CM7
|  /   /   /   /   |   /   /   /   /   |   /   /   /   /   |   /   /   /   /   |
  (H)     (H)        (SH)
```

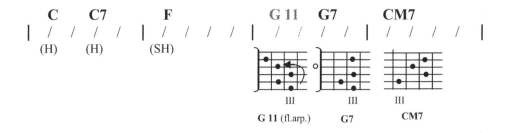

G 11 (fl.arp.)   G7   CM7

Rock and roll legend **Chuck Berry** struts his signature 'duck walk'
while playing his Gibson guitar, to the delight of fans, during a
1980 Hollywood, California, concert at the Palladium

III. CHROMATIC ALTERATIONS

They generally concern **minor chords** and especially **seventh chords**. It will consist, in these cases, in the alteration of the **fifth** and/or **ninth** notes of these chords, which will either be **"flattened"**, or **"sharpened"** depending on harmonic situations.
We discussed it earlier on, in the chapter on **altered 7th chords**.

But major chords can,also, be altered as we will see in the examples to follow.
The notes that will be altered, this time, will be the root - octave (**8**), the major seventh (**M7**) and the third (**3**).
It will be necessary to add to this list the polytonal chords (major or minor) whose use, in modern music, has not ceased to widen.

Here are some harmonic situations in which it is possible to encounter them:

1. Chromatic alterations of the SUBDOMINANT(IV) chord:

Substitution very often met in the Congolese Rumba, during the transition from the chord **IV** to the chord **I** as in the example below:

- Original progression :

```
   G   G7      C              C            G   Am    D            G
 | / / / /  | / / / /  | / / / /  | / / / /  | / / / /  | / / / /
   I(SH)  I7     IV(B)                       I(GB)  II(GH)  V(H)       I(SH)
```

- Substitution:

```
   G   G7      C              Cm           G   Am    D            G
 | / / / /  | / / / /  | / / / /  | / / / /  | / / / /  | / / / /
   I(SH)  I7     IV(B)———→     IVm (B) ——→I(GB)  II(GH)   V(H)        I(SH)
```

The third note (**3**) of the chord **IV** has been **"flattened"** to give a **IVm** chord before coming back towards the chord **I**.
Note the « **descending line** » on the 2nd string of the guitar from the **G7** chord.

2. Alterations of the minor chord of a II - V – I progression

As we already know, **the II chord** is naturally a minor chord in a major key.
The most encountered alteration will consist in the **"flatening"** of its fifth (**5**), generally performed on its extended form with a seventh note (**7**) to give the **m7^{b}5** chord.
But we could as well play the chord under its simple **m^{b}5** form.

Example:

- **Original progression :**

```
   Dm    G7        CM7
| /  /  /  / | /  /  /  / |
  (B)   (GB)      (B)
```

- **Substitution:**

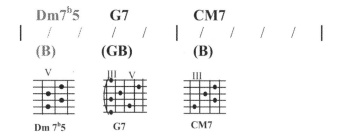

```
   Dm7ᵇ5    G7          CM7
| /   /   /   / | /   /   /   / |
  (B)    (GB)        (B)
```

Dm 7^{b}5   G7   CM7

* In the case where a minor chord is played on the whole bar, it will be possible to play the original minor chord on the two first bar beats and the altered minor chord on the two remaining bar beats, as below:

- **Original progression :**

```
   Dm              G7          CM7
| /  /  /  / | /  /  /  / | /  /  /  / |
  (B)             (GB)        (B)
```

90

- Substitution :

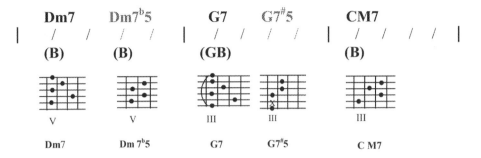

3. Creation of ascending or descending melodic lines:

It will be a question of alterating a given chord progression in order to create, for some reason, an **ascending** or **descending** melodic line by **semi- tones** (chromatic).
To make them well audible, we will preferably use the high pitched notes of these chords as below:

- Original progression :

```
     C      Am      Dm    G7      C
|  /   /   /   /  |  /   /   /   /  |  /   /   /   /
   (B)   (GB)      (B)   (GB)      (B)
```

- Substitution:

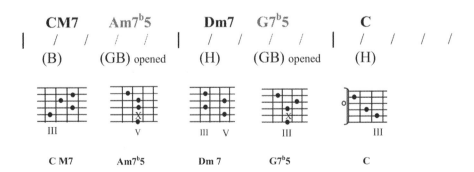

But it will be possible, just as well, to use the basse line for this purpose and in this case, **polytonal chords** are best used because they offer a better harmonic layout of chords.

These chords, as said earlier on, are triads with altered bass notes, and can therefore be considered as altered chords of some type.

Example:

- Original progression :

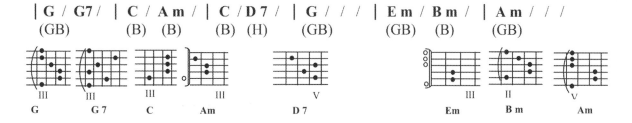

- Substitution :

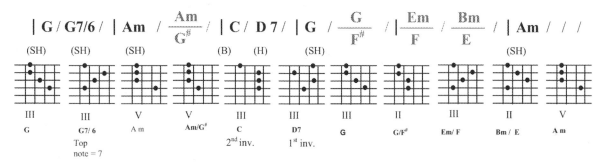

4. Single chord over several bars:

If a single chord is played over several bars, it will be left to the guitarist enough time to insert some melodic variations by creating **ascending** or **descending melodic lines** with chosen notes, but this time on single chord as follows:

- **Original progression :**

- **Substitution :**

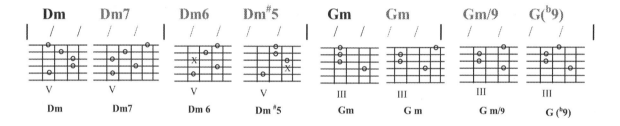

Another variant of the same technique, with major chords in harmonic position **I**, when the following chord is of position **IV**:

- **Original progression :**

```
       C               F
|  /   /   /   /  |  /   /   /   /  |  /   /   /   /
  (H)             (SH)
```

- **Substitution :**

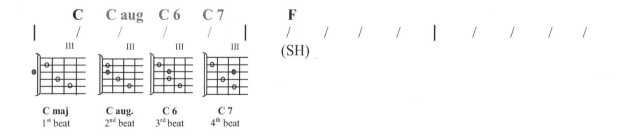

5. « Resolved » 7ᵗʰ chords

We stated principles related to them in a previous chapter.
They will therefore be very appropriate during the transition from chord **I** to **IV** and chord **V** to **I**, the two chords being separated by a fourth.
It is a question of transforming the original chord into an altered 7th chord or its altered extended chord .
The chords **I** and **V** (initial) could, moreover, be transformed into **dominant 7ᵗʰ** chords (or their exteneded forms) before being altered, according to the principle seen in the paragraph on the use of extended chord (pages 81-86).

Example 1:

- **Original progression** - Transition from **I** to **IV**

- **Substitution :**

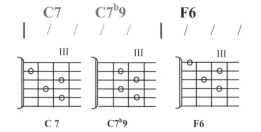

The altered seventh chord is played over the two last beats of the first bar.

Example 2 :

- **Original progression :**

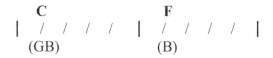

- **Substitution** :

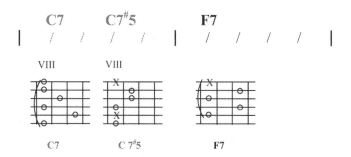

Example 3 :

- Original progression – Transition from **V** to **I**

| / / / / | / / / / | / / / / |
Dm ... **G7** ... **C**
II_m (B) ... V7(GB) ... I (H)

- Substitution :

Dm ... **G7** ... G7$^\#$5 ... **CM7**

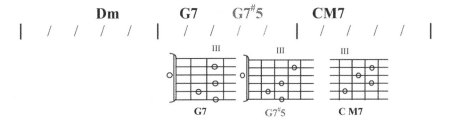

G7 ... G7$^\#$5 ... C M7

- Other possible Substitution :

Dm7 ... G9 ... G7^{b}9 ... **CM7**

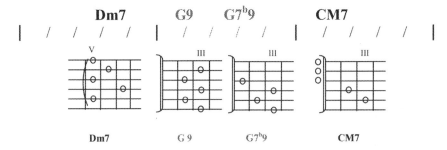

Dm7 ... G 9 ... G7^{b}9 ... CM7

Example 4 :

Original progression :

G ... **C**
(GB) ... (B)

- Substitution :

G7 ... G7^{b}5 ... **C7**

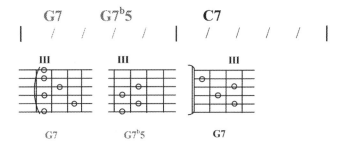

G7 ... G7^{b}5 ... G7

Example 5 :

- **Original progression :**

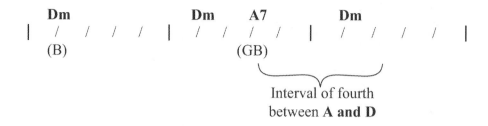

- **Substitution :**

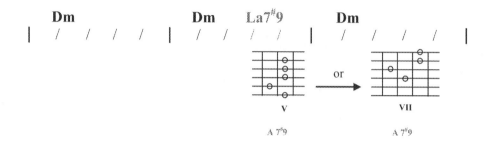

6. Dominant chord followed by another one located a semi-tone lower

When a **seventh** chord is followed by another chord constructed a semi-tone lower, the first one can be substituted by an **altered seventh** chord.

Example:

- **Original progression** - In the key of **G**

G	B	C	B
/ / / /	/ / / /	/ / / /	/ / / /
(SH)	(B)	(B)	(B)

- Substitution

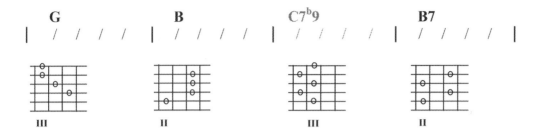

7. Other situations:

In all other case where the rhythm guitarist wants « **to match** » the lead guitarist melody line, when one of these altered notes is played by the latter.

IV. SUBSTITUTIONS BY A DIMINISHED SEVENTH CHORD

Rule 1: Any seventh chord can be substituted by a diminished 7th chord (dim) constructed **a semi- tone** below and vice versa .

Comments: this rule will also be applied, and in a very appropriate way, to 7b9 chords, which are "synonymous" with **diminished 7th chords** (see chapter on synonymous chords).
However by so doing, we should:

1. bear in mind one of the most interesting properties of **diminished 7th chords** seen in a previous chapter: they "reproduce" every 4 frets (1,5 tones) ascending or descending to the keyboard (see page 32).

2. pay attention to the **bass line** created by the substitution, which must follow the context of the song or, at least, remain the most musical possible.
Example :

- progression   II   V   I :

      II   V   I
      Dm   G7   C
| / / / / | / / / / |
    (B)   (GB)   (B)

Taking into account the above remark on the bass line, it will be necessary to avoid substituting **G7** by a diminished chord containing a bass note played on the 6th string.

Example :

It would create an altered bass note which will change the bass line not necessarily in a "musical " way.

Two possibilities of substitution will then be considered in that case:

1. Substitution by « **homonymous** » diminished 7th chords of barré shape (roots on the 5th string).

Two situations are generally encountered:

a) Keep the root of the chord **II**:

We will substitute **the 7th chord** by a **diminished 7th chord** whose root is the same than that of the **chord II**, but homonymous with the **V$^{\#}$ (diminished 7th) chord** as follows:

- **Original progression :**

```
    Dm      G7          C
|   /   /   /   /  |   /   /   /   /  |
   (B)    (GB)        (B)
```

- **Substitution :**

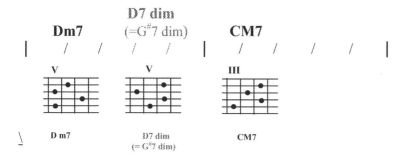

b) Play **another** homonymous diminished 7th chord (with the root located at 1,5 tone lower than the diminished 7th above) :

It will be a question of playing a diminished 7th chord of the same name, but at 1,5 tones lower , according to the property of "reproduction" mentioned earlier.
This chord will have its root at one fret (0,5 tone) lower than chord **I**.

- **Original progression :**

```
    Dm      G7          C
|   /   /   /   /  |   /   /   /   /  |
   (B)    (GB)        (B)
```

- **Substitution :**

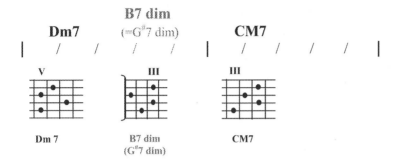

2. Substitution by a homonymous diminished 7th chord **of small barré shape** (root note on the 4th string).

Example:

- **Original progression :**

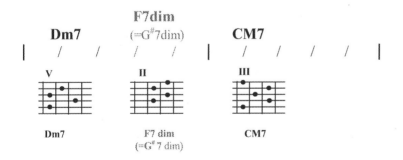

- **Substitution :**

Rule 2: When two successive chords of a progression are separated by an interval of **fifth or 3,5 tones** (in this instance, during the transition from **IV** to **I** and from **I** to **V**), the first chord can be partly substituted by a 7 dim chord.

As in the preceding case, we will have two possible situations (while paying attention to the bass line).

1. Keep the same roots: the **7 dim** chord will have the same root as the substituted chord.

- **Original progression :**

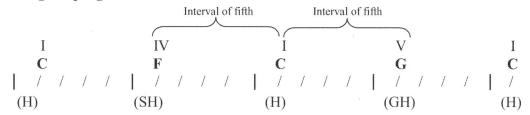

I		IV		I		V		I
C		F		C		G		C
/ / / /		/ / / /		/ / / /		/ / / /		/
(H)		(SH)		(H)		(GH)		(H)

- **Substitution :**

C C7		F F7 dim		C C7dim		G G7		CM7
/ / / /		/ / / /		/ / / /		/ / / /		/
(H)						(GH)		

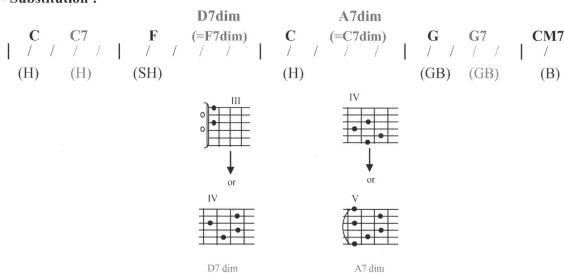

F7 dim   C7 dim

2. Play another 7dim chord (homonymous):

- **Original progression :**

I		IV		I		V		I
C		F		C		G		C
/ / / /		/ / / /		/ / / /		/ / / /		/
(H)		(SH)		(H)		(GH)		(H)

- **Substitution :**

		D7dim		A7dim			
		(=F7dim)		(=C7dim)			
C C7		F		C		G G7		CM7
/ / / /		/ / / /		/ / / /		/ / / /		/
(H) (H)		(SH)		(H)		(GB) (GB)		(B)

D7 dim   A7 dim

V. SUBSTITUTION OF THE ALTERED V7 CHORD OF A II V I PROGRESSION

We have seen that the chord V of a progression of the **II V I** type is "resolved" and can therefore be altered.

This altered V7 chord can be substituted by a **7th chord** (or even an **altered 7h chord**) constructed a **flat fifth** interval higher, that is to say **3 tones** higher.

We could therefore have the following successive substitutions in the key of **C** :

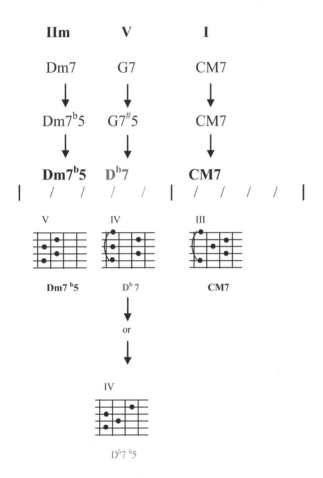

Remark: The **IIm** chord has also been altered according to the mode of substitution seen in paragraph 3 on chromatic alterations.

VI. SUBSTITUTION OF A V CHORD BY A m7^{b}5 CHORD (harmonic position VII)

We saw that in "Western" music, the chord in harmonic position **VII,** which is a **m7^{b}5** chord, is often replaced with the **V** chord in its first inversion. Conversely, we can also substitute a **V**chord of a progression by a **VII** chord, with the intention of getting some harmonic variation.

Example: in the key of C Maj.

- **original progression:**

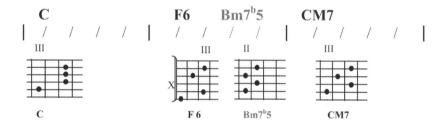

```
     I                IV    V        I
     C                F     G        C
|  /   /   /   /  |  /   /   /   /  |  /   /   /   /  |
   (B)              (GB)  (GB)      (B)
```

- **Substitution :**

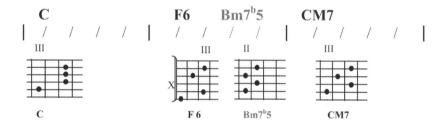

Note: The **VII** chord can, of course, replace the **V**chord partly, instead of substituting it completely, and create a «horizontal » substitution.

It will then be necessary, for example, to play the **V**chord on half of the time which was allowed for it and play the **VII** chord on the rest of the bar.

B. HORIZONTAL SUBSTITUTIONS

I. CHROMATIC APPROACHES:

1. Chords separated by a tone:

When **two neighbouring** (successive) **chords** of a progression are separated by a tone, a **chord similar** (with the same form and harmonic function) **to the starting chord** can be intercalated **to approach chromatically** (by a semi tone) the following chord .

Example 1 :

-Original progression   :

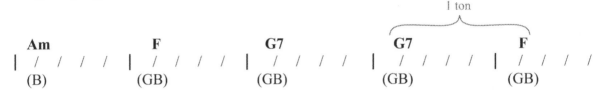

- Substitution :

Example 2 :

- Original progression :

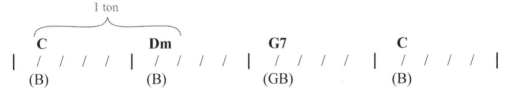

- Substitution :

2. Chords separated by more than a tone

If the two chords are separated by more than a tone, the following chord is chromatically approached by a chord **similar** (same form and harmonic function) **to itself**, this time.
It can be approached **from « above »** (semi-tone higher) or **from « below »** (semi-tone lower).

- Original progression :

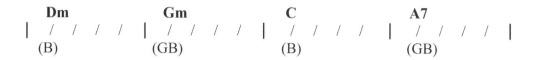

- Substitution :

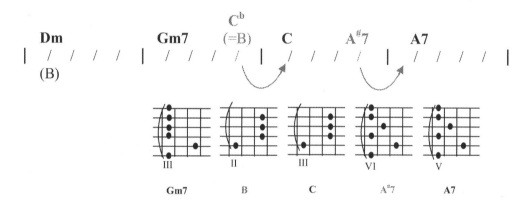

II. SUBSTITUTION BY ONE OR TWO RELATIVE CHORDS

1. Substitution by a relative minor chord (often, the primary relative minor)

The existing **major chord** is <u>partly replaced</u> (over 1 or 2 other beats of the bar), by its **relative minor**.
It is one of the the simplest and commonest substitutions, together with that of the previous paragraph.

- Original progression :

```
     C              F    G7      C
|  /  /  /  /  |  /  /  /  /  |  /  /  /  /  |
   (H)           (SH) (GH)      (H)
```

- Substitution :

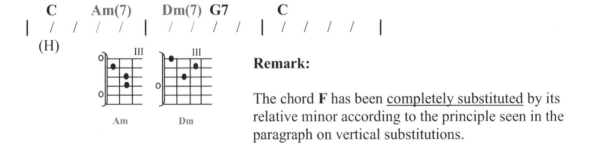

Remark:

The chord **F** has been <u>completely substituted</u> by its relative minor according to the principle seen in the paragraph on vertical substitutions.

2. Substitution by two relative minor chords (the primary and secondary relative minor):

The existing **major chord** is <u>partly replaced</u> with its **two relative minor chords**.

- Original progression:

```
     C                 C                 F                 G7                C
|  /   /   /   /  |  /   /   /   /  |  /   /   /   /  |  /   /   /   /  |  /
   (H)               (H)               (GB)              (GH)              (H)
```

- Substitution:

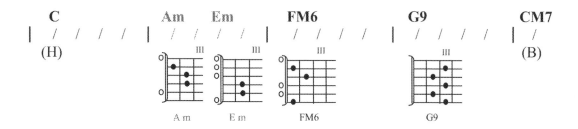

```
     C              Am      Em        FM6               G9                CM7
|  /   /   /   /  |  /   /   /   /  |  /   /   /   /  |  /   /   /   /  |  /
   (H)                                                                    (B)
```

* **Am** is the relative minor (primary) of **C** : **Am7** without root = **Cmaj**.
   Em is the secondary relative minor of **C**: **CM7** without root = **Em**

III. SUBSTITUTION BY MINOR «PASSING CHORDS»:

The **minor chords** of a given scale (or key) are **secondary chords** of this key (**IIm, IIIm** and **VIm**), while **the major chords (I, IV** and V) are the **main** ones.

These minor chords being secondary, can therefore be intercalated (one or several) **between two successive** (often major) **chords** of a progression «to embellish it».

- **Original progression :**

```
     C                 F
|  /   /   /   /  |  /   /   /   /  |
     I                 IV
```

- **Substitutions :**

a)
```
        C     Dm        Em    F
     |  /   /   /   /  |  /   /   /   /  |
        I     IIm       IIIm  IV
```

b)
```
        C     Am        Dm    F
     |  /   /   /   /  |  /   /   /   /  |
        I     VIm       IIm   IV
```

c)
```
        C     Em        Dm    F
     |  /   /   /   /  |  /   /   /   /  |
        I     IIIm      IIm   IV
```

*Sometimes these secondary chords are used to create some **«diatonic effects»** as below:

- **Original progression :**

```
     C              C              G7             C
|  /   /   /   /  |  /   /   /   /  |  /   /   /   /  |  /   /   /   /  |
     I                             V7             I
```

- **Substitution:**

```
  CM7   Dm7      Em7   E♭m7      Dm7   G7#5      CM7
|  /   /   /   /  |  /   /   /   /  |  /   /   /   /  |  /   /   /   /  |
  (B)   (B)      (B)   (B)       (B)   (GH)      (B)
```

IV. SUBSTITUTION BY THE CHORDS OF THE DIATONIC SCALE

Between two chords of a progression, it is possible to intercalate, if the "duration of the beat" allows it, **a group of chords of the diatonic scale** chosen according to the desired effect.

- **Original progression :**

```
    I                V7              I
    A                E               A
|  /  /  /  /  |  /  /  /  /  |  /
  (GB)            (H)
```

- **Substitution:**

```
    I    III m  IV   V7          II m
|   A    C#m    D    E7   |   Bm   /   E7   /   |   A
  (GB)   (B)    (B)  (H)      (B)      (H)         (GB)
```

V. SUBSTITUTION OF A 7TH CHORD BY A MINOR CHORD:

Rule: any **V7** chord of a key can be <u>partly replaced</u> or <u>preceded</u> (in the same bar) by the **IIm(7)** chord of the same key.
This **IIm** chord is moreover constructed **a fifth higher** than the **V7**.

- **Original progression:** in the key of **E maj**

```
    I                IV               V7               I
    E                A                B7               E
|  /  /  /  /  |  /  /  /  /  |  /  /  /  /  |  /
  (GB)            (B)            (H)            (GB)
```

- **Substitution:**

```
    I                IV               II m   V7          I
    E                A                F#m(7) B7           E
|  /  /  /  /  |  /  /  /  /  |  /  /  /  /  |  /
```

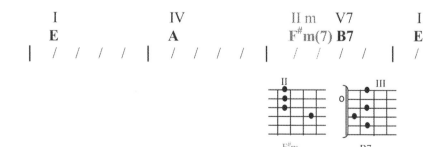

Comments:

1. Minor chords can be altered in substitutions.
The most encountered alteration is that of the **fifth** which will be **diminished** (^b**5**).

2. We have said, in the first part of this chapter (vertical substitution), that the **V7** chord could be substituted by a **VIIm7^{b}5** chord.

As a consequence of the two comments above, the previous example will become (this time in the key of **C maj**):

- Original progression :

```
      I                 IV                V 7                I
      C                 F                 G7                 C
|  /   /   /   /  |  /   /   /   /  |  /   /   /   /  |  /   /   /   /  |
     (H)              (GB)              (GB)              (H)
```

- Substitution :

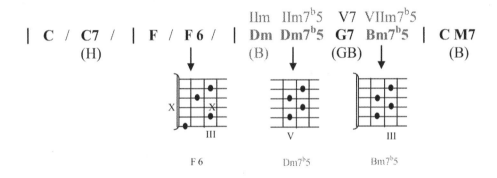

```
                             IIm  IIm7b5  V7  VIIm7b5
|  C  /  C7  /  |  F  /  F 6  /  |  Dm  Dm7b5  G7  Bm7b5  |  C M7  |
      (H)                         (B)        (GB)              (B)
```

F 6   Dm7^{b}5   Bm7^{b}5

Photo of **Django Reinhardt**

VI. SUBSTITUTION BY CHORDS FOLLOWING THE « CYCLE OF FIFTHS»:

a) Substitution of a 7th chord by another 7th chord constructed a fifth higher :

Rule: Any dominant seventh chord (**V7**) can be preceded by another **7th** chord constructed a fifth higher. .

Example 1 :

- **Original progression :**

```
    I                IV               V7               I
    C                F                G7               C
|  /   /   /   /  |  /   /   /   /  |  /   /   /   /  |  /   /   /   /  |
  (H)              (GB)             (GB)             (B)
```

- **Substitution :**

```
    C    C7          F                D7    G7         CM7
|  /   /   /   /  |  /   /   /   /  |  /   /   /   /  |  /   /   /   /  |
  (H)  (H)        (GB)             (H)   (GB)        (B)
```

If, for any reason, the accompanist stays on the **V7** chord over several bars, this rule can be extended by substituting another **7th** chord (**A7**) also constructed a fifth higher than the chord coming from the previous substitution (here **D7**).
We can repeat this process at leisure, as long as "time" allows it, to get a « series of substitutions » as follows :

- **Original progression :**

```
    C    F           G7                                                    C
|  /   /   /   /  |  /   /   /   /  |  /   /   /   /  |  /   /   /   /  |  /
    I    IV          V7                                                    I
```

- **Substitution :**

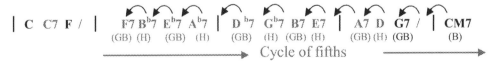

```
| C   C7  F  /  |  F7  Bb7  Eb7  Ab7  |  Db7  Gb7  B7  E7  |  A7  D  G7  /  |  CM7
                  (GB) (H)  (GB) (H)     (GB) (H) (GB) (H)    (GB)(H)(GB)     (B)
```

Cycle of fifths

This sequence of chords recreate,**backwards** ,what is called in music the « **CYCLE OF FIFTHS** » which is widely known under the form below:

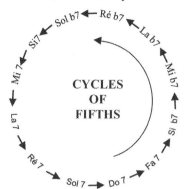

By reading it counter-clockwise, every chord is constructed a **fifth higher** than the following one.

The guitarist who has "worked " enough on his instrument will be able to master all their positions on the fingerboard and reproduce them easily.

Remark: as we will see it below, the chords of the cycle can also become **minor sevenths (m7)**. We could just as well use **7th altered chords**.

b) Alternation of minor and 7th chords while going back up the cycle of fifths:

We have seen that a **7th chord** could be substituted (preceded) by a **minor chord (or m7)** constructed a **fifth higher** .Conversely, a **minor chord (m7)** can be preceded by a **7th chord** constructed **a fifth higher :**

- **Original progression:** in the key of **C**

I	IV	V7	I
C	**F**	**G7**	**C**
/ / / /	/ / / /	/ / / /	/ / / /
(H)	(GB)	(GB)	(B)

- **1st Substitution :**

C	F	Dm7 G7	C
/ / / /	/ / / /	/ / / /	/ / / /
		(B)	

As seen previously, **G7 (V7)** is substituted by a minor chord (**Dm7**), constructed a fifth higher.

And **Dm7** can, in turn, be substituted by a **7th chord** constructed **a fifth higher,**here,A7 :

- **2th Substitution :**

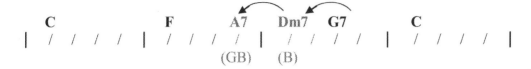

We can therefore embellish a music piece by playing around with substituting <u>alternately</u> **seventh** and **minor** chords, while going back up the cycle of fifths (=BACK CYCLING) :

- **Original progression :**

- **Substitutions :**

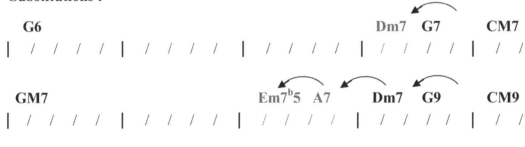

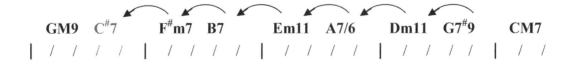

We can, in conclusion, generalize this principle to all kinds of chords (meaning chords of any harmonic functions) and state the following rule:

« Any chord can be substituted (preceded) by a **seventh chord**, or even **altered seventh chord**, constructed a **fifth** (3,5 tones) **higher** than its root».

Example 1 :

- **Original progression :**

     Dm7   **G7**   **CM7**

| /   /   /   / | /   /   /   / |

- **Substitution :**

    A7   **Dm7** **G7** **G7$^{\#}$5**   **CM7**

| /   /   /   / | /   /   /   / |

Example 2 :

- **Original progression :**

     DM7   **Em7**

| /   /   /   / | /   /   /   / |

- **Substitution :**

    A7^{b}9   **DM7**   **Em7**

| /   /   /   / | /   /   /   / |

Example 3 :

- **Original progression:**

```
    C7                    F7
|   /   /   /   /  |   /   /   /   /  |
```

- **Substitution :**

```
   G7#5     C7           F7
|   /   /   /   /  |   /   /   /   /  |
```

VII.VARIATION FROM A SINGLE CHORD OVER SEVERAL BARS

When in a music piece, there is a sequence where a single chord is played over several bars, it will leave enough time to the guitarist to exercise his creative imagination.

He could, for instance, have a good time creating ascending or descending sequences of chords as follows:

- **Original progression:**

```
    C
|   /   /   /   /  |   /   /   /   /  |   /   /   /   /  |   /   /   /   /
```

- **Substitution :**

```
   C    CM7      Dm7    Em7        FM9    C9/6      CM9
|   /   /   /   /  |   /   /   /   /  |   /   /   /   /  |   /   /   /   /
```

or

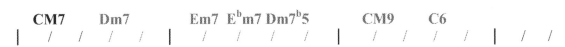

```
  CM7      Dm7        Em7  E♭m7 Dm7♭5      CM9      C6
|   /   /   /   /  |   /   /   /   /  |   /   /   /   /  |   /   /
```

VIII. SUBSTITUTION BY DIMINISHED SEVENTH CHORDS or any other chord with " diminished characteristic"

In the first part of this chapter (vertical substitution) we mentioned the unique characteristic of the diminished seventh chords which **repeat or reproduce themselves every 4 frets** (upwards and downwards the fingerboard).

It has as a consequence that there are only **3 different diminished 7th chords in every key**.
In practice therefore, it means that whatever chords you choose, it will always be possible to find a diminished 7th chord that "matches" the substitution progression.

That is why the diminished 7th chords are the most used and usable chords in common substitutions.
They can, indeed, be intercalated between any kind of chords.

For example during the transition from **C (I)** to **G (V)**, all the 3 different kinds of diminished 7th chords can be used with more or less "satisfaction" according to the desired effect :

-Original progression :

```
    I                V
    C                G                    C
|  /   /   /   /  |  /   /   /   /  |  /
   (H)              (GH)
```

- Substitution number 1 :

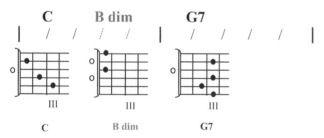

- Substitution number 2 :

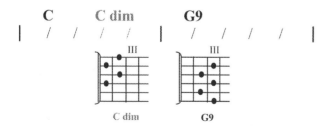

- Substitution number 3 :

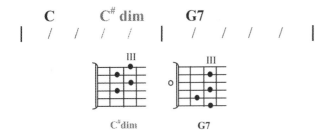

* This situation is often encountered when 2 successive chords of a progression are separated by an interval of fifth, in this case during the transition from the **I** chord to the **V** and from the **IV** to the **I**.

We will then have the following chord sequences:

- **I** - **I**$^{\#}$dim - **V**

- **IV** - **IV**$^{\#}$dim - **I**

However, diminished 7th chords are more frequently used in **chromatic substitutions**, with the intention of creating **descending or ascending chromatic melodic lines** in the progressions:

- Original progression:

CM7　　　Dm7　　　Em7　　　Dm7　　　CM7
| / / / / | / / / / | / / / / | / / / / | / / |
(B)　　　(B)　　　(B)　　　(B)　　　(B)

- Substitution :

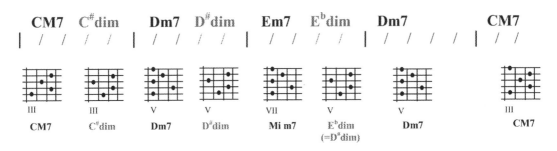

Other example with Grand barré chords: in the key of **G**

- **Original progression :**

| **G** | | **Am** | | **Bm** | | **Am** | **D7** | **G** |

| / / / / | / / / / | / / / / | / / / / | / / |

- **Substitution :**

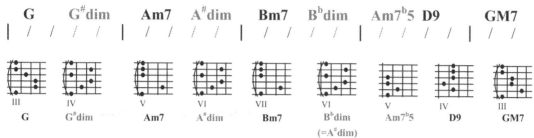

| **G** | G#dim | **Am7** | A#dim | **Bm7** | Bbdim | Am7b5 | **D9** | **GM7** |

| / / / | / / / | / / / | / / / | / / |

III   IV   V   VI   VII   VI   V   IV   III

G   G#dim   Am7   A#dim   Bm7   Bbdim (=A#dim)   Am7b5   D9   GM7

*The altered 7th chord of a progression of II V I type can also be partly substituted by a diminished 7th chord constructed a semi tone lower, as follows:

- **Original progression :**

Dm7   **G7b9**   **CM7**

| / / | / / | / / / / |

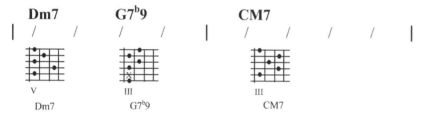

V   III   III

Dm7   G7b9   CM7

- **Substitution :**

Dm7b5   **G7b9**   G#dim   **CM7**

| / / | / / | / / / / |

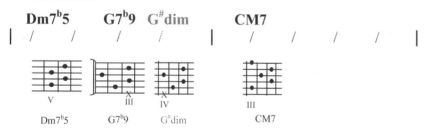

V   III   IV   III

Dm7b5   G7b9   G#dim   CM7

Comment: the bass line, in the substitution, should be the most musical possible. Reason why the chords **G7b9** and **G#dim** were played without their respective root notes on the 6th string, therefore in inversions (see X).

Note also that the chord **G7b9** played without root note, resembles the chord **Bdim**. (see synonymous chords).

As we have just said, we saw in the chapter on synonymous chords that the **7ᵇ9** chord was synonymous with the **diminished 7th chord** (page 74).

As a result the **7ᵇ9** chord will also have a property "similar" to diminished 7ᵗʰ chords, that is to say **to reproduce a "similar" chord**, but not identical, **in every 4 frets (1,5ton)** upwards and downwards the fingerboard.

That is also true for **<u>any chord having a «diminished characteristic»</u>**, namely the **7ᵇ5, 13ᵇ9, 13ᵇ5, 7ᵇ5ᵇ9** etc... including the **m7ᵇ5** chord.

Example 1:

- **Original progression:** Resolved chords

- **Substitution :**

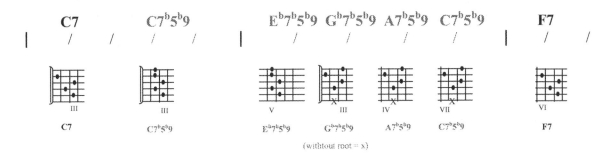

(without root = x)

Example 2:

- **Original progression:** Progression **II   V   I**

| **Dm7**   **G7**   **C**
| /   /   /   / | /   /   /   / |

You will remember that we have said earlier on that the **m7** chord of a **II - V - I** progression will have its fifth « flattened » during a substitution, to give the **m7^{b}5** chord.
As a result, by this property, similar to diminished chords, we will have :

- **Substitution :**

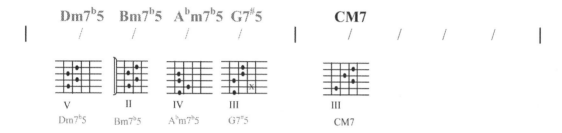

IX. SUBSTITUTION BY AUGMENTED CHORDS

It is made in the same way as with diminished chords but with the only difference that **these chords reproduce or repeat themselves in every 5 frets** (instead of 4) on the fingerboard.

Example:

- **original progression:** Resolved chords

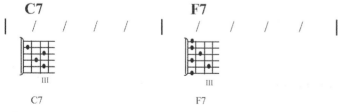

- **Substitution :**

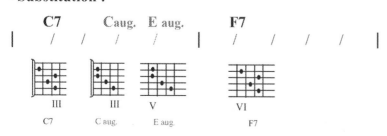

X. SUBSTITUTION BY NEW DOMINANT CHORDS

This kind of substitution is a «horizontal variant» of the cases described in the first part of this chapter.

It is about either the case of a **resolved 7th chord** or a **dominant chord followed by another one located a semi-tone lower.**
 In both cases, we will partly substitute the initial chord by a **new dominant chord** constructed **3 tones higher**.
This new chord could, of course, be "extended" or altered according to the desired effect.

Example 1: **Resolved chords**

- Original progression :

- Substitution 1 :

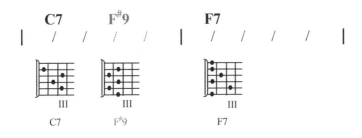

- Substitution 2 :

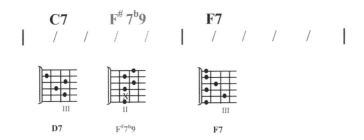

Example 2: **Dominant chord followed by another one, a semi-tone lower.**

-Original progression :

G	**B**	**C**	**B**
	/ / / /	/ / / /	/ / / /	/ / / /
(SH)	(B)	(H)	(B)

- Substitution :

G	**B**	**C** F#7b9	**B7**
	/ / / /	/ / / /	/ / / /	/ / / /

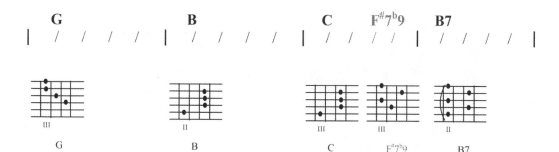

| G | B | C | F#7b9 | B7 |

BB King performs at the Glastonbury Festival at Worthy Farm,
Pilton on June 24, 2011 in Glastonbury, England

CHAP.VII. <u>THE BLUES</u>

We would not have found this work to be complete without speaking about the BLUES which is a particular music style, which gave birth to ROCK and JAZZ without however, itself, disappearing.

I dare imagine that if the creators of the BLUES had learnt to read music, they would not have created this tremendous music style which revolutionized its domain.

Not knowing how to read and write music and having only their musical ear, talent and inspiration as guides, these blacks of America succeeded in creating a style which did not follow any conventional musical criterion of that time: this universal artistic monument.

Indeed, the harmonic structure of the "traditional" Blues differs from the modal and harmonic structures of the conventional major and minor scales.

This particular characteristic is due to the facts that:

1. A Blues chord progression is almost entirely constituted of 3 **basic chords** (main chords) **of a major key** that is to say the **I, IV, and V.**

2. The chords are therefore **major** and, very often **seventh**.

3. They move by **intervals of fourth**

4. The sequence of chords follows a **constant cycle** of either **12** or **8 bars**.

5. Its rhythm is particular: **"Shuffle"** and use of **triplets**.

6. The lead guitarist uses a particular scale to improvise: **pentatonic minor scale**.

✳ As the chords used here are often seventh chords, all the techniques of **extension**, **substitution** and **alteration** of 7th chords described in the previous chapters could be applied , although **the dissonance of these seventh chords is never really resolved.**

By so doing, the traditional Blues will then be progressively transformed, in its structure and sound, to become what is called the «**BLUES - JAZZ**»

Examples of traditional Blues progressions :

1.12-bar blues progression (4 beats each), in the scale of **C** :

```
1       2       3       4
‖ C (7) | C(7)  | C(7)  | C 7 |

5       6       7       8
| F (7) | F(7)  | C(7)  | C (7) |

9     10     11     12
| G7  | F(7) | C(7) | G7        ‖
                     12  or
                     | C (7)    ‖
```

2. **Variation** (often encountered) of the progression above :

```
1       2       3       4
‖ C (7) | F(7)  | C(7)  | C (7) |

5       6       7       8
|  F (7) | F(7) | C(7)  | C (7) |

9   10     11     12
| G7 | G7  | C(7)  | C(7)       ‖
```

3.8-bar blues progression :

```
1       2       3       4
‖C (7)  | C (7) | F(7)  | F(7) |

5       6    7           8
|  C (7) | G7 | C(7)-F(7) | C(7)-G7        ‖
```

* HARMONIC TRANSFORMATION of the traditional Blues into the Blues - Jazz:

We will take as an example a **12-bar** progression in **A**:

- Original progression:

```
1        2        3        4
‖ La 7  | D 7    | La 7   | La 7   |


5        6        7        8
| D 7   | D 7    | A7     | A 7    |


9       10       11       12
| E 7   | E 7    | A 7    | E 7        ‖
```

1. Chord substitution :

- Some **7th chords** will be partly substituted by **m7 chords**: bars **4,9-10** combined and **12**.

- Some other **7th chords** could be partly substituted by **diminished chords**: bars **5** and **6** combined.

- Some **m7 chords** from the previous substitutions could be altered chromatically: bar **12**.

2. Chord extension:

Some chords could simply be "extended".
That will concern the **non resolved 7th chords** (bars **1,2,3,5,7,8,** and **11**) and the **m7 chords** derived from the substitutions (bars **4** and **10**).

3. Alteration of resolved 7th chords:

3. Alteration of resolved 7th chords:

Bars **4**, **10** and **12**

So therefore, the traditional Blues progression will finally become :

- Substitution:

1	**2**	**3**	**4**
A 9	D9	A13	Em9 – A7^{b}9

5	**6**	**7**	**8**
D7/6	D$^{\#}$7dim	A9	A13

9	**10**	**11**	**12**
Bm9	E7$^{\#}$5	A13	Bm7^{b}5 - E7^{b}9$^{\#}$5

* Some guitarists will even be able to insert a **M7** chord in the bars **7** and/or **11** (**AM7**) or else in the bar **2** (**DM7**).

Many other kinds of substitutions can still be introduced, like: **7th chords** or **altered 7th chords** built a **fifth higher** (cycle of fifths) or **chromatic approaches** with **seventh chords** and etc… It will be more a matter of personal taste and inspiration.

In any case, have a good time …

- Original progression: BLUES in C

1 C7	**2** F7	**3** C7	**4** C7
‖ / / / /	/ / / /	/ / / /	/ / / /	

5 F 7	**6** F7	**7** C7	**8** C7
/ / / /	/ / / /	/ / / /	/ / / /	

9 G7	**10** G7	**11** C7	**12** G7
/ / / /	/ / / /	/ / / /	/ / / / ‖

- Substitution :

1 C7   G^b7   **2** FM7   Fm7   **3** Am7   D7   **4** G7   C7   G^b7

‖ / / / / | / / / / | / / / / | / / / / |

5 F7   F9   **6** F[#]dim   **7** CM7   **8** A7

| / / / / | / / / / | / / / / | / / / / |

9 Dm9   **10** D^b7   **11** CM7   Am7   **12** Dm7^b5   G7^b9

| / / / / | / / / / | / / / / | / / / / ‖

Harmonic analysis:

1. **M7 chords**: bars **2** (first two beats), **7** and **11** (first two beats)

2. **Cycle of fifths**: bars **3,4** (first two beats), **11** (two last beats) and **12**.

3. **Chromatic approaches**: bar **1** (from **G^b7** to **FM7**)
                                   bar **4** (from **G^b7** to **F7**)

4. **Extension of chords** : bars **5** and **9**

5. Substitution by a **7dim chord** built a semi- tone higher: bar **6**

6 **Resolved seventh chord**: bar **12** (from **G7^b9** to the **C7** of the beginning of the progression).

7. **Relative chord** (with major third): bar **8**

8. Substitution of a **7th chord** by a **minor chord** : bar **9**

9. Substitution of a **7th chord** by **another one,** constructed a **flat fifth higher** : bar **10**.

Author Biography

Dr Williams, medical doctor by profession but also talented and skilled guitarist with more than 30 years of experience.

Very young he started playing the guitar and singing in various bands while being exposed to many musical styles and genres ranging from jazz, rock rumba, bolero to reggae and pop music.

After exchanging his guitar for the stethoscope, he still found the opportunity, through this book in 2 volumes, to share his long experience and passion for the guitar.